CHURCH STAFF ADMINISTRATION

PRACTICAL APPROACHES

CHURCH STAFF ADMINISTRATION

PRACTICAL APPROACHES

(Successor to *Building and Maintaining a Church Staff*)

Leonard E. Wedel

**Foreword by
Reginald M. McDonough**

BROADMAN PRESS
Nashville, Tennessee

To My Wife
Nita

Foreword

It has been correctly stated that a church will not exceed the quality of its leadership. No segment of leadership effectiveness is more crucial than the church's employed leaders. This is true if a church's pastor is the only staff member or if the church has a large staff group.

The major strengths of the book in its original and revised form are twofold:

1. It presents a clear, concise, and step-by-step approach to church staff administration.

2. It gives a complete system of staff administration from the formation of a personnel committee to perform its evaluation. It is a practical how-to resource that will help a church begin a new staff administration plan or update an existing plan.

Although some staff groups have problems because of interpersonal problems, many staffs function poorly because of ineffective recruiting, orientation, and performance evaluation. Wedel's many years of experience in church and denominational personnel administration make his counsel in these matters invaluable.

An impressive fact about this revision of Wedel's original book is that he has done more than just update the original facts and figures. He has included information related to significant developments in staff administration that have developed since his first book was published. His discussion of personal goal-setting is an example of a significant addition in this revision.

Staff organization continues to change as churches search for patterns that fit very unique needs. This book not only presents traditional patterns but also includes the program director concept that is being used by an increasing number of larger churches.

I am pleased to recommend this book as a good edition to every church administrator's library. I have known Mr. Wedel for the fourteen years that I have served at the Sunday School Board and respect him as a person who loves the Lord, stays up-to-date in his field, and practices what he preaches in his own church work. The revised manuscript is a needed and welcomed resource.

REGINALD M. MCDONOUGH

Contents

1
How to Select
New Employees

The church-paid staff is made up of one or more employees who are engaged in supporting the work of the church.

The pastor serves as the chief administrator.

In a smaller church the pastor may be the only paid worker. He not only takes care of the pastoral ministries but serves as program director as well. He does a lot of things.

He may lead the congregation in singing, prepare and duplicate the church bulletin, order the church literature, and type his own letters.

When the work of the church begins to grow, he discovers he and his wife cannot do everything. He needs help. His first move is to enlist volunteer office help in addition to the volunteer custodian already on board.

As the church continues to grow, it becomes necessary to employ a part-time secretary and a part-time custodian. Later, a part-time music director is added to the staff to assist the pastor. And still later a full-time combination education-music person is employed.

When a church employs full-time professional workers, the promotional paperwork increases. So the church needs more office help.

Practically every church begins and grows a staff in the way described above.

Much later, a multiple staff emerges. The pastor continues to serve as the chief administrator of the staff in addition to his prime responsibilities in pastoral ministries. The pastor, however, has additional support through one or more workers who have been assigned supervisory responsibilities in addition to their other duties.

For example, the minister of education may supervise one or more office workers in addition to age-group and specialty workers. He may also supervise the hostess, custodian, and maids.

In other similar size churches the business administrator may be assigned the responsibility to supervise the financial secretary, hostess, custodians, and maids and clerical workers not directly related to the office of the minister of education. The minister of music may supervise the work of a part-time organist, pianist, and secretary.

In some larger staffs, the educational secretary may have the responsibility of supervising clerical workers related to the office of the minister of education.

In larger staffs another level of supervision has been established in the title of staff administrator, program coordinator, or program director. This person is responsible to the pastor for managing the staff's functions of program ministries, secretarial and clerical support, food services, equipment operation, and maintenance of buildings and grounds. He is usually responsible for all the business aspects related to the church. The supervisors of the various functions work with the program director in planning, organizing, directing, coordinating, and evaluating their work. See Exhibits VI and VI A for samples of staff organization charts.

Although paid staffs of churches may vary in size, their purpose is to perform tasks that support and sustain the five common functions of a church: to preach the gospel; to worship; to educate the members; to perform church ministries, and to apply.

The church's mission is the staff's mission. The church's goals are the staff's goals.

This concept places a grave responsibility on the pastor and other supervisors to lead staff workers to reach and maintain high levels of workmanship and interpersonnel relationships.

The pastor is not separate from the staff team, but is a member of it. At times he gives leadership, guidance, and direction; at other times he follows the counsel and suggestions of other staff members.

The blending of knowing how to lead and how to follow is basic to growing and developing a staff team.

Most pastors and other staff supervisors want to be a part of a well-managed staff. So do the secretaries, receptionists, clerks, and custodians.

Building and maintaining a well-managed staff begins by getting the right person for each job. The quality, dedication, and morale of the several members who comprise the paid staff contribute greatly to the overall attainment of a church's goals.

Quality shows in a number of ways—evidence of spiritual concern and a genuine desire to serve.

Quality shows in other ways. Letters neatly typed and framed on the page speak well of a church. Attractive church bulletins, either printed or duplicated by office machines, create favorable and positive attitudes of members toward the church's total program. Accurate office and educational records provide incentives to volunteer workers who have Sunday record-keeping duties. The receptionist creates goodwill for the church when she receives visitors, members, and vendors cordially and helpfully.

Goodwill is also created when staff workers follow through on promises they make to church members. An entire staff is sometimes affected adversely when one paid worker is careless about following through on commitments. For example, one church had a paid worker who usually said, "Yes, I'll do that," but seldom did. Church leaders were confused and frustrated when they found the kitchen unavailable after it had been promised for a certain time; or the room assigned was not cleaned and arranged; or the church doors were locked when a meeting had been scheduled; or educational supplies were not purchased; or needed workers had not been enlisted.

All in all, the paid staff can affect the general attitude and optimism of the entire church. The church, then, has a vital interest in the quality and dedication of its staff workers. The pastor and other staff supervisors, with the help of the personnel committee, have the responsibility of obtaining the best possible workers.

What is involved in the selection process?

The three main areas for consideration are recruiting, screening, and placement.

The overall selection process may involve several personal interviews with one or more applicants, the giving of typing, shorthand, and other tests, the following up of business and character references, and the evaluation of all the accumulated information before the final decision is reached to employ or not to employ a certain person.

Some supervisors chafe under what they describe as a tedious selection process. They devise shortcuts. After sizing up a person only a few minutes, they feel infallibly guided by some intuitive sense—"She is what we're looking for," or "She isn't."

Both men and women are afflicted with this snap judgment disease. The best cure is to keep in mind some of the deplorable mistakes made along the way. Some persons who were expected to succeed failed; others who were expected to fail succeeded—somewhere else!

Even after a thorough checking of an applicant's qualifications, one may vacillate between two choices: to employ or not to employ. The reference follow-ups, test scores, and interviews affirm the applicant's potential. Still one hesitates until the pressures of mounting work push him to a decision.

The dilemma may be compared to the middle-aged couple who asked the banker for a loan. He was dubious. However, the wife supported her husband's request so convincingly the banker agreed. After the husband signed the note and got the money, she turned to the banker and said, "You're a lousy judge of character."

Sometimes employment decisions prove to be misjudgments. However, in spite of the varying degrees of confidence or anxiety about making a decision, it must be done.

How do you go about finding a qualified replacement when a vacancy occurs? One supervisor said, "First, if the person who left us was 'tops,' I'd go somewhere and cry."

Although this feeling of regret is normal, the supervisor must give immediate attention to finding a qualified replacement.

Some supervisors fall into self-devised traps by insisting on "finding another person just like Louise." This is wishful thinking.

What he may mean is that now he has to assume some of his own tasks that he had assigned to Louise. Or he will miss all the extra things Louise did for him and his wife, such as deposit his check, make personal purchases, pay his bills, baby-sit at his home occasionally, and sometimes buy his family's weekly supply of groceries. Or Louise was the only one in the office who always agreed with him on any idea he proposed. Or Louise was an excellent worker and a good team member.

A sobering thought to consider about replacement is: Suppose someone or some committee of a church looked for a person exactly like some predecessor. If a successor is selected on that basis, how can he possibly perform as two people? And yet, somehow, a "Louise wall" is unintentionally built when a replacement is being sought. The opposite opinion, "We don't want another Louise, that's for sure," may be just as bad. How then should replacements be secured?

A sensible and positive approach is to consider the church's interest, to find a person who best fits the job requirements. Believe it or not, a new worker may have some traits and abilities superior to any former worker.

First, review the continued need for this job or for this kind of job. Positions do change over a period of time. It's possible some of the present duties are obsolete or could be combined with another similar job. Don't perpetuate a job just because it exists.

Second, restudy the job requirements. This is a good rule to follow after each termination. Plan a conference with the worker a week or so before termination. Go over every aspect of the job— what is done regularly, occasionally, and infrequently. Later, as notes about the job are studied, needed changes in work assignments affecting the work of other persons in the office may be discovered. Review the suggested changes with the other employees and ask for their comments and ideas. You may or may not wish to incorporate all of their suggestions in the revised job description.

Third, check to see if the vacancy is a promotion possibility for a worker in the office. If so, promote the person who meets the qualifications; then seek a replacement for the new vacancy.

Fourth, check the file of applications completed by prospects during the past several months. If none qualifies, look through the names of the church roll, unless, of course, job qualifications preclude their consideration.

The placement bureau or state employment office in your town or city may provide some leads. The local business college is another recruiting source. For some church jobs, high school graduates with or without business experience are another source. Sometimes the businessmen in the church membership are able and willing to give helpful information. A pastor or minister of education of another church may be able to furnish the name of a prospective applicant.

When talking to others about the vacancy, be sure to describe briefly the job duties and qualifications. To say that a secretary's job is open in the church is misleading. The word *secretary* means different things to different people. For some, it means the highest paid office job in the church. For others, it may mean the person who keeps the educational records.

Sometimes an applicant learns of the vacancy through friends, neighbors, the paid staff workers, or church members. The applicant may call by telephone to ask for more job information. If he is interested, invite him to the office for further talk.

When a job is vacant for a few weeks, some supervisors get panicky and in desperation employ a person who does not meet the job requirements. The better practice is to employ a temporary worker during the interim period, or to get volunteer office help from church members.

What tools are helpful in the selection process?

• *Prepare an application form.* The application form includes a variety of questions designed to get factual information about an applicant.

Decide what basic information is wanted about each applicant. Generally, application forms include questions covering personal data, education, employment history, skills, experience, health, and references. You may wish to include a section on church affiliation and activity. See Exhibit 1 for a sample application form, for use by secretarial-clerical-manual applicants, and Exhibit 1A, a data sheet for use by professional applicants. The data sheet, if not completed prior to the "call" to the church should be completed as a part of the orientation session. The completed forms become a part of each employee's personal folder.

Although few persons may ask about a job in the church, still an application form is well worth having. Ask each applicant who comes into your office to complete this form. When there is a vacancy, the completed applications on file will serve as ready references. After six months or so, applications on file are of little value, so update the files. Write the applicants and request them to indicate their continued interest on an enclosed, self-addressed card.

• *Prepare reference follow-up forms.* The application form usually includes space for the applicant to name at least three people who have known him for several years and space for him to write in any prior work experience.

One of the important phases of the total selection process is to make a full investigation of the applicant's background and job experience through a series of meaningful reference checks.

The person who conducts the original interview is responsible for making reference checks. The person or persons called or visited, from whom information is sought, will respond more openly to the original interviewer than anyone else.

Reference checking is not a job to be delegated to a secretary or clerk even though this person may be highly qualified in her field of work.

The best way to gather information about a professional candidate is to visit the person who can supply it. This method may be costly. However, the cost may be inconsequential when compared to the substance of information obtained.

The telephone is the next best way to check references. See Exhibits II and III for sample telephone questionnaire forms to use in work and character reference checking.

The interviewer follows his prepared guide during the telephone inquiry. He avoids asking leading questions. He listens for clues in addition to the actual information received such as hesitation or seeming reluctance to answer some questions, uncooperative attitude, or too glib. Look For FreeDom/Easyness/Security and Flexibility

The least reliable method is to write references for information. See Exhibit IV and V for sample work-character questionnaire forms.

Written character references especially are not too reliable. A person usually hesitates to write his candid opinion about an applicant who has named him as a character reference, especially if the information is negative.

Written business letter follow-ups usually give more specific, factual, and useful information.

The investigative process is time consuming; especially so when it involves candidates who are to fill professional positions on a church staff.

A thorough investigative job is no guarantee that the best qualified person will always be selected. However, the probability level is enhanced considerably.

A slipshod job of reference checking may occasionally produce a windfall. But the risk is too great. The wrong person may create a problem for the staff as well as for the church.

• *Prepare job descriptions.* The prospective employee should receive accurate and complete information as to the duties of the job under consideration. See chapter 4 for a detailed presentation of this subject.

* *Establish job qualifications.* The purpose of establishing job qualifications is threefold:

To serve as a guideline in the selection process

To ensure consistency in the employment process

To serve as a support when pressures are made to employ an unqualified person

Suppose there is a clerical vacancy in your church office. What kind of a person should you look for? To what extent would such things as age, clerical skills, experience, education enter into the consideration? Job qualifications or job specifications serve as guidelines to help in the selection of the most qualified person for the job.

In many churches vacancies occur infrequently. Nevertheless, a list of job qualifications is important. Even one termination in several years makes a set of qualifications a welcome support.

The following questions may prompt ideas that will help you in setting up a church's job qualifications for each staff position description.

What are the minimum educational requirements for the various jobs on the staff?

What minimum typing speed is required for each clerical job?

What minimum shorthand speed is required for the jobs of stenographer or secretary?

How much experience is required, if any?

What health and/or physical requirements, if any, should be established?

Several advantages are provided by church-approved job qualifications: (1) the preliminary interview can be performed more quickly; (2) an applicant can be dealt with more straightforwardly and encouraged or discouraged in pursuit of a job in the church; and (3) refusal to a church member, parent, or a prominent church leader who wishes employment of a person obviously not qualified for the job is supported.

A church policy covering job qualifications loses its effectiveness when exceptions are made. For example, a supervisor in one church employed an office worker whose membership was elsewhere— an exception to the policy. A year later he interviewed a person for another office job vacancy. He explained that if the applicant were employed, she would be required to join the local church. She replied, "Why should I? You have a person on your staff who is a member of another church." It is doubtful the supervisor presented a convincing rebuttal.

Another staff supervisor learned about exceptions the hard way. The applicant seated before him met all job requirements except typing speed. She typed approximately thirty words a minute which was less than required for the job. After explaining the required skill for the job to the applicant, she pleaded, "If you'll only give me a chance, I'll increase my speed on the job." With the understanding that she would improve her typing skill, the supervisor agreed to employ her. Six months later very little improvement was evident.

In the meantime, the other clerical workers in the office were patient and helped the new girl get started. However, they soon became aware that her lack of typing skill affected adversely several areas of work flow. They wondered why the supervisor would employ a person who couldn't "cut the mustard"—and who could blame them!

On the other hand, it is possible to establish minimum job qualifications so high and rigid that finding replacements becomes difficult. For example, to require a college degree, or even one or two years of college, for a clerical job may narrow considerably the field of applicants. Another problem eventually surfaces when a worker is over-employed. He loses interest in the job and may become a problem to his supervisor. Establishing job qualifications is a significant part of the screening process.

It is important that every supervisor on the church staff follow whatever qualification guidelines are established. The paid staff creates serious problems for itself when each supervisor—pastor, minister of education, minister of music, business administrator—has his own set of job qualifications.

• *Prepare employment policies.* Another tool to aid the personnel committee and/or the staff supervisor is to establish written employment policies. The following questions, which cover several areas of policy, may be helpful.

Should the church employ both husband and wife on the regular payroll? If so, should one be permitted to supervise the other?

Should the church employ a relative of a present staff worker?

If so, under what conditions?

Under what conditions would the church reemploy a former worker? salary? tenure? benefits?

Should the church reemploy a staff retiree? If so, under what conditions? wage or salary? part time? full time? temporary? time limit?

Is a worker required to be a member of the church? another church of like denomination? or does church membership make any difference?

What are the minimum and maximum age limits, if any, under and over which the church will not employ?

Although churches are exempt from the federal legislation passed in the mid-sixties regulating hiring practices, it is appropriate to present the import of the law here for information.

Title VI and VII of the Civil Rights Act prohibits discrimination on the basis of race, color, national origin, religion, marital status, and sex. The Age Discrimination Act of 1967 prohibits discrimination on the basis of age, specifically those persons between forty and sixty-five years of age.

The state employment agencies are specifically bound by the law. If you use their services for applicant referrals, your job order request includes three items: job qualifications, job duties, machines used.

• *Define employment classifications.* You need to know the type of employment you are offering a prospective worker—whether it is regular, part time or temporary. The applicant wants to know his employment status before he is placed on the job.

• *Establish a salary plan.* One of the purposes of setting up a formal salary plan is to give accurate salary information to the prospective employee. See chapter 5 for a detailed presentation of this subject.

The tools for selection provide a support for the next three important steps:

Preparing for the interview
Conducting the interview
Evaluating the interview

How do you prepare for the interview?

Generally, every staff supervisor has the responsibility of filling approved secretarial, clerical, and manual job vacancies under his supervision. At times, he may get counsel and assistance from his pastor and the personnel committee. How you proceed depends on your staff administration policy.

The pastor and the personnel committee usually recruit and screen the professional workers on the church staff such as the minister of education, minister of music, and so forth. Sometimes a special committee is appointed for this purpose.

The minister of education, for example, is usually asked to sit in with the personnel committee and make suggestions during the recruiting and screening steps involving a staff candidate which he, the minister of education, would supervise.

Some staff supervisors have observable deficiencies when it comes to interviewing a job applicant. Regardless of where a vacancy exists on the church staff they excuse their failure to use acceptable interview preparation techniques largely because of day-to-day job pressures. Or that infrequent job vacancies dull the use of their interviewing skills repertoire.

In churches with multistaff organizations, the need for improving interviewing techniques is becoming more apparent. Any deficiencies on the part of the interviewer can be corrected through a planned program of self-improvement. Numerous books on how to interview are available in city libraries.

One of the two high orders of supervisory judgment is the selection of qualified personnel. The other is the objective evaluation of an employee's job performance.

The place to begin in preparing for the interview is for you to review in detail qualifications of the job in question. Make certain you have correct information of salary and benefits. If available, review the applicant's resumé or completed application form and reference checks.

In the process of preparation you consider inputs to the job required of the employee rather than desired outcomes of work performance. To accomplish this approach, you prepare a list of skills, proficiencies, and attitudes which appear crucial to the job under consideration.

1. You determine the skills required to perform the job. Below is a partial list of skills covering a variety of church staff jobs.

Custodial   Delegation
Receptionist   Conference leading

Machine operation   Communications
Specialized technical knowledge   Human relations
Analytical   Supervisory

2. You list the proficiencies required by the job. Below is a partial list.

Physical ability   Planning ability
Creative ability   Organizing ability
Physical health   Promotion ability
Read and write   Verbal facility
Grammar–spelling   Intellectual ability
Pleasing voice   Preparing and delivering talks
Social ability   Flexibility

3. You determine the attitudes required for the job. Below is a partial list.

Acceptance of one's role and status in the staff organization
Readiness to relate to and communicate with one's supervisor
Willingness to relate to and cooperate with co-workers
Willingness to abide by the church's and staff's work policies and procedures
Willingness to adjust work hours when emergencies arise

Your next step is to decide which items in 1, 2, 3 above, along with those you have included, have priority consideration for the job in question. You recognize that none of the applicants is going to fill all these requirements. You are aware also if the job requirements are too exacting, you may not find any qualified applicants. Conversely, if the job requirements are ill-defined, your interview may be sketchy and your selection decision faulty.

You prepare notes containing your list of priority job qualifications. Although in the interview you may not be able to determine precisely the degree of strength or weakness of each qualification inherent in the prospect, you will process a great deal of pertinent information to guide you in making a selection decision.

You should read the applicant's application and/or resumé prior to the interview session. You should prepare notes and questions as spin-offs of the application. You should be well enough prepared so that a glance at your notes during the interview will continue to keep you on track.

If possible, arrange an appointment with the applicant. Schedule a time which is mutually convenient. If the applicant is already employed, schedule the interview during his free time. In most cases professional candidates are invited to the host church for an extended session with the pastor and the personnel committee. The steps in preparing for an interview apply to both office and manual workers and professional workers.

Planning ahead for the applicant before he arrives assures the productive use of interview time. Preparation, then, gives the supervisor solid support for the interview and a sure way to start a good relationship with the prospective employee.

How much interview time should you schedule?

There is no universal formula for setting a certain period of interview time. Each job, depending on the skills, proficiencies, and attitudes to be explored, determines its own time frame. An interview with a candidate to fill a clerical vacancy would not require as much interview time, for example, as a session with a professional candidate who is being considered to serve as minister of youth. This fact does not mean that some workers on the church staff are second-class persons because they hold lower salary rated jobs. As persons, they are first-class.

However, the dramatic difference in job titles may prompt some supervisors to depreciate the value of the interview planning process for clerical and maintenance jobs. Nothing could be more disastrous to the total team work concept of a church staff when the hit or miss interviewing process results in employing job misfits. The entire staff is affected adversely.

How do you conduct the interview?

The interview can be a pleasant and profitable experience or it can be dull and drab for both participants. How the interview moves depends largely on advance preparation and the ability of the interviewer.

An interview is a social interaction, but not a social visit. It is a conversation directed to a definite purpose. It is a free exchange of information based on goodwill directed toward finding the person best qualified for the job. A productive interview establishes a friendly relationship, gets, and gives information.

The main purpose of the interview is to assess those skills, proficiencies, and attitudes in applicants that contribute to job success.

Some applicants do not make an appointment. They walk in and expect someone to talk to them. Do so, if at all possible. Instruct your secretary, in such instances, to receive the applicant cordially and request that the person complete the application form, assisting as necessary.

You should review the application form prior to interviewing the "drop-in" applicant. Obviously, you have not had time to plan adequately for the interview. If the preliminary interview reveals employment potential for an available vacancy, you should schedule a second interview a day or so later to give time for completion of the investigative process. Qualified applicants for some areas of church staff work are hard to find so don't wait too long to schedule the second interview.

If you are not available to interview the "drop in" applicant, ask the secretary to receive the completed application form, thank the person, and inform him a follow-up contact will be made in a day or so. Be sure to follow through on the contact commitment even though no vacancies presently exist.

Keep in mind that both parties to the interview are experiencing first impressions about the other. Sometimes the interviewer feels because he is in the "driver's seat" he is the only one adding up first impressions. It may be interesting and surprising to learn later, after the person is employed, what his first impressions were of the interviewer who may now be his supervisor.

First impressions, however, may or may not be reliable. They are based on limited information and could be a trap for the unwary interviewer. In this same vein you must be aware of your stereotypes, know and control your own biases and predilections.

The following suggestions may be helpful in conducting the interview:

• Schedule an appointment. It is usually a matter of mutual convenience. However, don't schedule interviews toward the close of the day. You may have last things to do and be tempted to cut short the interview time.

• Keep the appointment. Not only keep the appointment, but be on time! An appointment is akin to a personal pledge—a promise.

If it is impossible to be present at the specified time, ask the secretary to tell the person waiting about the delay and of the expected time of return.

Or, if you are in your office but tied up on a project which must be finished in ten or fifteen minutes, ask the secretary to explain the brief delay. Or, better yet, walk out of the office for a moment to meet the person, apologize for the delay, and tell him that the interview will take place in just a few moments.

• Another important item is to tidy up the desk. A cluttered desk, or one piled high with papers—even though in neat stacks— may make the applicant feel that he is intruding on your work time. Also, if you know yourself to be a "pencil-on-desk-tapper," you should place pencils and pens out of reach.

• Greet the applicant warmly. Make him feel welcome. Open the interview by conversing briefly and informally about some subject of mutual interest. Information on the application form usually provides good leads. Not many applicants are "old hands" at job interviewing. They are nervous, sit stiffly, and are usually somewhat frightened. Opening remarks can do much to relax both of you. Keep in mind the purpose of the interview is to get the applicant to talk freely and to volunteer information related to education, past experience, and so forth.

• Move into the body of the interview by covering some of the items and questions on your notes. Keep in mind the purpose of the interview is to discover to what extent the applicant's skills, proficiencies, and attitudes mesh with the requirements of the job under consideration.

You ask questions that call for narrative responses which can reveal information about the applicant's work habits, attitudes concerning previous work experiences, human relations skills, and personality, to name a few. Of course, during the interview the applicant usually puts his best foot forward.

Some example inquiries are:

"If you could have changed things at your high school (college-seminary) what would you have changed first?"

"Describe a typical day (or week) on your present or previous job."

"In what way were you required to work with others to get your job done?"

"What things did you learn on your previous job?"

"What would be the ideal job for you?"

"What are your personal interests in life?"

• Give the applicant undivided attention. This is not always easy to do, especially when there are time or job pressures. The applicant quickly senses any disinterest when you shuffle papers, or write yourself a note, or answer the telephone, or fidget with pen, pencil, or some desk gadget.

The best way to give attention is to listen to what he says. Then follow-up questions are more pertinent. Also, you are more alert to what is not said.

• Answer questions. Before the interview is terminated, ask the applicant if he has any questions. It is important to observe the kind of questions asked. They can say a great deal about a person. However, do not automatically "blackball" a person because he asks poor or wrong questions.

• Conclude the interview courteously. Express appreciation to the person for interest in a job in the church.

Tell the applicant whether he does or does not qualify for the job. Generally, people appreciate the facts. Do not give employment hope to a person who does not qualify by concluding the interview with a remark such as, "We'll call you if we need to talk with you further."

Some supervisors try to ease the applicant's disappointment by talking in platitudes for several minutes. Meanwhile, the applicant knows by the tone of his voice and weak closing statements what he is trying to say. Most people prefer that the interviewer omit the wasted words and get to the point.

Getting to the point does not mean that you abruptly say, "You just don't qualify for the job." Rather, it means reaching a conclusion in the same warm and friendly spirit which pervaded the entire interview.

On the other hand, give the applicant encouragement if he seems to qualify for the job vacancy. Tell him that a follow-up will be made on previous work record and references before the next interview. Discuss briefly the salary of the job if the applicant is a good prospect. Salary is usually an unspoken question in the mind of the applicant. Salary information will help him decide the extent of his interest in the job which may later be offered.

Ask the applicant to take a typing speed test before leaving (or whatever tests the job requires). Suggestions on administering tests are given later in this chapter. There may or may not be time to score the tests before he leaves.

What are some common interviewing errors?

• Asking leading questions. This leads the applicant into answers you seem to want. Examples of leading questions are: "You did like your previous supervisor, didn't you?" "You must have liked your previous position very much." "You feel like the church staff would be a good place to work?"

• Using to an excess annoying and redundant expressions such as "as I read you," "I see," "of course," "very good," or similar phrases. You may not be aware of these repeated expressions until you tape several of your interviews.

• Doing too much of the talking. Talk little. Concentrate on listening. Talk only enough to keep the conversation informal and friendly. Avoid expressing opinions or telling personal experiences.

Some interviews are a disappointment to the applicant because the interviewer talks mainly about his job, or family, or the hard time he had getting an education, or about his hobbies. Seemingly, every contribution the applicant makes to the interview prompts a recall of the interviewer's experiences.

• Attempting to be clever in your questioning. Do not try to angle the applicant into a trap. Do not intentionally confuse or embarrass the applicant. The key word during the interview is *relationship.* It is difficult, if not impossible, to establish goodwill through cleverness and trickery. Being less than your best is a reflection on the integrity of the church you represent.

• Assuming the role of teacher, parent. The applicant may need advice—even ask for it—but don't give it. Giving counsel is not the purpose of the interview.

• Putting the applicant under pressure by deliberately questioning his responses or by disagreeing with what he says. Obviously, the use of this interviewing error shatters goodwill quickly and makes a shamble of the interviewing session.

• Asking questions or making statements which provoke a feeling of antagonism. Generally, this error occurs when you arbitrarily declare your word on subjects discussed as final. Some examples are:

"I wouldn't have a secretary who couldn't type eighty words a minute. What do you think?"

"What do you think of pantsuits in a church office?" And after she answers in the positive, he replies, "No secretary of mine will wear pantsuits in the office." Then he adds, "I feel the same way about short skirts, tight sweaters, chewing gum, and socializers."

Some interviewers are fanatics about certain things. It shows in the interview session especially when the interviewer is not prepared in advance. Or it shows if he is prepared but lacks control over his feelings.

• Asking more than one question at a time, such as "You say your previous job was in Hometown? What did you do there? I mean, what jobs did you have and when did you leave to go to college and what college did you attend?" Obviously, the applicant, who is attempting to adjust to a strange situation, may become even more unsettled and confused when you ask a continuous series of questions.

• Talking without communicating. Some interviewers and some applicants feel that they must keep the conversation moving by talking. This concept is opposed, of course, to the purpose of communication.

The purpose of effective conversation is for the person receiving the information to understand it exactly as it was transmitted by the sender. Especially is this purpose pertinent to the interviewer who, during the interview, will not only transmit from time to time questions and information to the applicant but will also receive information from the applicant. See chapter 8 for additional information on communicating.

• Losing control of the interview. Sometimes a knowledgeable applicant reverses the questioning technique and begins questioning the interviewer. You should be alert to what is happening and resume the burden of questioning the applicant.

You should, however, tell the interviewee that part of the interview period will be devoted to questions he may wish to ask. This supports openness and that you are willing to give information.

Nothing establishes your confidence more securely than when you know you have the interview situation under control.

How do you evaluate the results of your interview?

Immediately following the interview session check your notes and questions and record comments made by the applicant. Evaluate your overall impressions of the applicant. You should ask yourself these questions:

• Did I follow my preinterview plan?

- Was I prepared for the interview? Where could I improve?
- How much more do I know of the applicant than appears on the application form?
- Was the interview more perfunctory than personal?
- Was the applicant satisfied, seemingly, with the interview?
- Did I fall into any bad habits such as asking questions which are recorded on the application form? talking too much? expressing opinions? failing to listen? and so forth.

What additional actions relate to the selection process?

- Conduct the second interview. The second interview, and perhaps a third in some cases, is arranged only if you are more than casually impressed with the applicant's potential. The purpose of this interview is to:

Review the applicant's file

Review results of tests, if any

Ask questions gleaned from reference follow-ups. (Do not reveal to the applicant the reference follow-up statements. This is confidential information.)

Review salary information

Discuss employee benefits

Offer him the job

Set a date for the applicant to report for work.

- Test for job skills. Results of typing, shorthand, and other clerical tests provide additional information for help in determining the employability of an applicant. Tests cannot measure what a person *will* do on the job; only what he *can* do. An indiscriminate use of tests is not recommended.

Most churches do not have staff members who are schooled in the use of tests. Some churches, however, are located in cities that have a state employment office. This office will serve without charge. Make the acquaintance of an official and learn of these services. When an applicant is employable, refer him to the employment office for typing and other tests.

If a church is located in a city or town which does not have these testing services, typing and shorthand tests can be given in the church office.

For typing speed tests, use material from a typing manual or prepare copy. Copy consists of accurately pretyped material of moderate word difficulty. In the white space on the right-hand margin of the copy write in the running total of the number of strokes in each line of type. Add the total of each line to the one following. For example, the first line may have 62 strokes, counting characters and punctuation (but not spaces between words). The total number of strokes in the second line may be 64, making the figure in the margin to the right of the second line 126 (62 plus 64). Continue figuring the running line total. The figure in the right-hand margin of the last line may be 4,355 (or whatever).

Give the applicant an opportunity to practice several minutes on the typewriter to be used for the test. The test copy for the applicant should not show the line stroke totals. They should appear only on the master copy which is used for scoring. A speed test usually is ten minutes long. Give the starting and finishing signals.

To grade the test follow these five steps:

(1) Jot down the total strokes typed.

(2) Divide the total strokes by five (average number of strokes per word) to get the gross number of words typed.

(3) Divide the gross number by ten (ten-minute test) to get the gross number of words per minute.

(4) Count the errors. Proofread the test copy carefully, placing a circle around every misspelled word, omitted punctuation, omitted word, strikeover, and so forth. Count the circles for the total errors.

(5) Subtract the total number of errors from the gross number of words per minute in (3) above to get the net number of words per minute.

Suppose an applicant typed 2,980 strokes in ten minutes with five errors. The computation according to the five steps above, would be as follows:

(1) 2,980 strokes

(2) 596 gross number of words typed in ten minutes (2,980 divided by 5)

(3) 59.6 or 60 gross number of words per minute (596 divided by 10)

(4) 5 errors

(5) 55 net number of words per minute (60 minus 5).

A typing score of 40–50 words per minute is fair; 50–60 is good; above 60 is average. Give the applicant another test if he thinks he can improve his score.

To give a shorthand test, dictate to the applicant two or more 100–150 word letters prepared for this purpose. The letters should compare with the kind normally dictated. The supervisor may need to practice his dictation speed to make it between 80–100 words per minute. He might time himself on the following 100-word letter (Include inside address).

Dr. Harold Jones
Denomination College
College Town, USA
Dear Mr. Jones:

I accept your kind invitation to speak to the students and faculty on October 6 on the occasion of the college's twentieth anniversary.

Thank you for sending along a copy of the latest yearbook. I reviewed it with a great deal of interest, especially since three of our own young people are students at Denomination College.

Your willingness to meet me at the airport is certainly appreciated. However, Mrs. Gregory and I plan to make the trip by car.

I'm looking forward to this assignment. Thanks for asking me.

Sincerely,

Observe the applicant's shorthand speed and general ability. Assign a typewriter and request a transcription of notes. Record elapsed time for the transcription. Divide the total number of minutes into the total number of words dictated to get an average words-per-minute score. A score of 15–25 words-per-minute is average.

Observe also the finished product—the typed letters. Are they framed well on the page? Is the left margin even? Is the right margin fairly even? Are there strikeovers or messy erasures? Would one be willing to sign his name to these letters for mailing?

Give the applicant an opportunity to try again if the first transcription test is not acceptable. A strange environment often keeps a person from performing at his best.

One may wish to assign the giving and scoring of typing tests to a secretary in the office. Perhaps the dictator should give the shorthand test.

• Select the qualified applicant. To evaluate the qualifications of people is a fine art and requires a high order of judgment. In some instances it is clear, after interviewing two or three applicants, which person is most acceptable. In other instances, when applicants have similar qualifications, the decision is more difficult to make. The interviewer may base his decision on positive reactions resulting from the overall screening process.

He may ask himself questions such as: Who is best qualified in terms of needed skills? Who would fit the best with the other office workers? Who seems to be most alert? Who has the best ability to express himself? Who seems most self-confident? Who seems to have the best health?

A good supervisor makes every effort to eliminate personal prejudice from his employment decisions. A few of the common prejudices are color of hair, posture, eyes close together, protruding chin, large ears, the way the hair is cut or groomed.

Prejudice usually creeps into one's personality makeup so gradually he is surprised to learn of its presence. A person should study his areas of prejudice. They may be a hindrance to the intelligent selection of people for jobs in the church.

2
How to Help
the New Staff Member
Get a Good Start

Most people have either pleasant or unpleasant memories of their first day on a job. If you had an unpleasant experience, chances are you would feel, upon reflection, that your frustrations could easily have been avoided if better induction planning had been done by your supervisor.

For example, when one minister of education was asked to relate his first day's experience, he said:

"The pastor was out of the city in a revival meeting. I didn't know my way around and was not even sure of the location of my office. Much of that first day I spent walking through the church facilities. I introduced myself to the janitors, the maid, and met the workers in the church offices. But I wasn't sure which persons, if any, I would supervise. Of course when the pastor returned, he showed me around and answered my questions. Since then he has given me excellent counsel, help, and support. But I'll never forget the frustrations I felt that first day."

Another staff worker had a different reaction: "I recall the first day as a very pleasant experience. The pastor took time to give me a personally conducted tour of the church buildings and grounds as well as of the church's mission. He introduced me to all the workers, then showed me my office which was clean and ready to move into. After lunch together we spent two hours in the pastor's office. He showed me the church staff organization chart, reviewed my job, and explained my supervisory responsibilities. I felt that I got off to a good start."

When asked to recall their first day at work, several office workers made these comments:

"My first day was pleasant. The supervisor introduced me to

all the workers and arranged for one of the girls to go on break and to lunch with me. He showed me my work place and got me started."

"The supervisor showed me my desk and then excused himself for a conference. I sat there like a log for three hours with nothing to do. I tried to look busy. I finally got a *Young People's Quarterly* and started typing one of the lessons. Was I ever frustrated!"

"From the very first day my supervisor has never called me by my right name."

"On the first day he led me to believe I would get a salary increase in six months. I finally got one after fourteen months."

"I was made to feel wanted and needed. The supervisor talked to me as if he had all day, and I know he had loads of work to do. He was friendly, helpful, and interested in my making good on the job."

A good program of employee induction—helping the new worker get a good start—should provide a thorough introduction to the overall work of the church and the staff so that he may understand the framework in which he operates.

What should you include in an induction plan?

With some adaptations to fit the particular needs of professional, office, and maintenance workers the induction plan includes several or all of the following items.

- A tour of the church's facilities
- An introduction to all staff workers
- An explanation of employee benefits
- Complete information of the church's personnel policies, procedures, salary plan, pay dates, work hours, and so forth
- A review and explanation of job duties
- Information as to how the paid staff is organized to carry out the church's programs and ministries
- A brief overview of how the church operates through its deacons, church council, church committees, and so forth
- A brief review of the church's history
- A review of the church's programs, ministries, calendar of activities, schedule of services
- A tour of the community
- A visit to the church's mission(s), if any

Who is responsible for inducting the new worker?

The person on the church staff who will supervise the work of the new employee is responsible.

What induction preparation should you make?

Foremost, you must reexamine the significant role you play in helping a new worker get a good start. A careless or perfunctory attitude on your part during the induction process could dampen a new worker's enthusiasm and affect subsequent performance adversely.

You should prepare a tailored plan to fit the employee and his job. In some cases one or more of the suggested areas listed above might not be appropriate to include.

A day or so before the new employee reports for work be sure that his office and desk are clean. The desk should be stocked with an assortment of supplies neatly arranged. A new worker should not be expected to clean the desk or work space of a former employee.

Be sure a disconnected telephone is reinstalled before the new worker arrives. Do everything possible to make the physical arrangements supportive of mutual goodwill.

You must plan to be in your office not only the day of induction, but also when the new worker arrives for work.

Every positive impression supports the new worker's feeling "I know I'm going to enjoy working here."

Schedule ample time for the induction. Arrange your own work schedule to allow time for unhurried and uninterrupted talks.

Induction time the first day might include two or more hours in the morning with a similar time allotment in the afternoon. Keep in mind that it is difficult for a new employee to absorb the whole "bale of hay" at one sitting. Spreading out the information over a week or two may be necessary in some cases to cover fully and clearly all areas of the induction plan.

What do you include in an induction schedule?

An induction plan usually covers several hours of parts of one or two weeks, depending on the type of job involved. Below is a suggested schedule. Some of the suggestions may not be pertinent to all new workers, but they may help to develop individual plans—

one for the professional members and one for the office and maintenance paid staff workers.

Be sure to give the new worker an opportunity to ask questions
or make comments at any point in the induction process.

First day
• The purpose of the first day's orientation is to give the new
worker sufficient information about the church staff and his own
particular job to make him aware of his teamwork role.
• Be in your office when the new worker arrives.
• Greet him cordially and make him feel at ease. He wants to
be welcomed to a job—not thrown into it. A new worker usually
comes to the job with keen anticipation—a desire to make good;
to give his best. Your job is to stimulate, not to deflate. The first
three months are critical for a new worker. Therefore, give him
the attention he needs—not just the first day but throughout his
work career at your church.
• Assist him to complete forms required to place him on the
payroll—such as income tax, insurance, hospitalization, pension,
and so forth. Ask the financial secretary, if any, to assist.
• Show him his office or work place and where to hang his
coat and hat.
• Explain the day's work schedule including rest breaks, lunch
hour, and so forth.
• Review his salary, pay dates, and when he is eligible for consideration for his first salary increase.
• Explain the church's salary plan and its administration. Give
the employee a copy of the plan, if available.
• Take him on a tour of the church's facilities; show him where
to park his car.
• Introduce him to all staff workers.
• Review his duties and give him a copy of his job description.
• Get him started on the job; show how it should be done
and tell him why.
• Designate someone, if appropriate, to look after the new
worker socially at least the first day to take him to rest break and
to lunch.
• Follow up with him later in the day to offer any help or answer
questions.

Second day

The purpose of the second day's induction is to review the items presented on the first day and to enlarge the worker's concept of the administration of the church staff.

• Give him an opportunity to ask questions about the previous day's activities.

• Review the employee benefit program. This might include benefits such as vacation, holidays, pension, hospitalization, insurance, revival meetings, attendance at state and convention-wide meetings, and housing allowance and car expense, if any.

• Give him a copy of the organization chart of the paid staff and show him how his job is related to the total staff work. Explain staff relationships.

• Explain the church's personnel policies.

Third day

The purpose of the third day's orientation is to answer questions and to explain how the church carries on its internal administration and its outreach through programs and ministries.

• Give him an opportunity to ask for further information or clarification of his duties or of any item discussed previously.

• Explain how the church is organized to perform its work; include the deacons, church officers, church committees, as well as the educational organizations.

• Review briefly the church's history.

• Review the church's constitution and bylaws.

• Check employee's work. Comment and instruct as appropriate.

End of the first week

The purpose of this stage of the orientation is to acquaint the new professional worker with the church's field of work and related points of interest in the city.

• Give him an orientation to the community in which the church is located. Take time to tour the area pointing out churches, shopping centers, schools, medical services, public transportation routes, public libraries, service agencies, and so forth.

• Visit the church's missions, if any.

First paycheck

• Hand him his first paycheck; explain the deductions.

• Discuss his work progress. Ask how he thinks he is getting along. Answer his questions. Give constructive help.

• Give him a chance to share his ideas about how certain tasks may be done. Some of the best ideas for work and facility improvements come from new workers.

After the first paycheck, then what? Is the new employee now on his own?

Not entirely. For one thing, you need to follow up frequently during the early stages of his employment. There are always problems to be solved during the learning phase of a job. The new worker needs your encouragement and support from time to time. This requires a genuine interest on your part to help the new employee make good.

What other responsibilities, if any, do you have to the new worker?

Actually, your job to train and develop others is never finished. The first six months for a new employee are most important. He learns many things. He develops good or bad work habits. You are always close by to encourage, commend, counsel, and instruct. Your role is to help people develop their potential.

As the weeks and months pass, you should continue to observe the work of all those for whom you are responsible and to take whatever remedial action is necessary. You should:

• Observe such things as repeated tardiness, frequent absence, failure to adhere to rest period and lunch hour schedules. Infractions are usually indicators of job disinterest, personal or home problems.

• Check quality as well as quantity of work performed.

• Check work habits.

• Discuss work problems at the time they occur.

• Encourage improvement. Assist the worker in his goals for self-development.

What are the results of a good worker induction plan?

Good supervisors know that a plan for induction, training, and follow-through drastically reduces the time needed by new employees to become skillful and productive.

The chart below shows how a good induction plan can cut down the time it takes to get a new worker in full production.

CHART SHOWING HOW A GOOD INDUCTION PROGRAM CAN CUT
DOWN THE TIME IT TAKES TO GET AN EMPLOYEE IN FULL
PRODUCTION

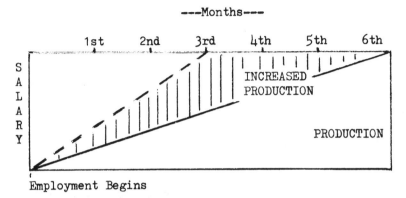

According to this chart, it takes six months for a new worker to attain full production status on a certain job. A thoughtful question is "how can I improve my job orientation plan to get a person into full production in less than six months?"

Let's presume that three months is the goal. In the chart the church is presently paying a worker full salary for six months. Part of the salary is for learning and training time and part for actual production. But why pay six months for learning and training time if it can be reduced to three months? If accomplished, the church is the beneficiary of full production in three months instead of six months.

Note the gradual increase in production during the six month's schedule compared to the rapid increase in production in the three months' schedule. In both cases the salary is unchanged, making a good case to reduce job training time.

A good induction plan has other benefits:

• Reduces turnover; new employees do not get discouraged and quit.

• Develops in the workers a sense of pride to be associated with the church.

- Gives workers a feeling of confidence.
- Develops morale.
- Provides stature and recognition.
- Builds teamwork.

However, now and then a person on the staff develops a poor attitude, is uncooperative and difficult to work with, and turns out shoddy work.

A good case for dismissal? Before a conclusion is reached, you should review your role as supervisor.

You are responsible for the performance of your workers, for helping them to attain their highest possible potential. Along with this responsibility goes commensurate authority to properly and reasonably direct and stimulate the workers to perform their jobs as efficiently as possible.

Workers who are allowed to fail in their tasks can never be used by you as an alibi. The responsibility for getting the job done rests more on you than on the worker.

When lack of interest, unrest, continued poor performance, repeated tardiness, excessive absenteeism, or other faults are evident, you must take immediate action to correct these failings or take alternate steps to dismiss the worker.

For example, assume a dismissal situation. Over a period of months each instance of job failure was discussed with the worker. Further, you communicated unmistakably that you expected immediate improvement. Assume, also, that the worker did understand that his work performance was not satisfactory. Based upon these assumptions, termination may be the best solution.

However, some situations not involving work fault may require immediate dismissal. Such offenses include theft, dishonesty, falsification of records, to name a few.

Some supervisors are reluctant to face up to their responsibilities in a dismissal situation. They know what they ought to do but just cannot get around to it. They employ a variety of delaying tactics, hoping the situation will improve or go away. Or that the worker will resign on his own initiative.

Dismissing a worker is an unpleasant task. Both lose; the dismissed worker and the church. There are times, however, when the church, through its staff, must take this action.

What steps are involved in dismissing an employee?

• Discuss the matter thoroughly with the pastor. Go over the file of recorded work faults and related conferences. The file should include incidents, violations, remedial conferences held, and dates. You and the pastor should be in agreement. Sometimes the pastor, who has not been close to the situation, wants to wait a while, to put it off, to try something else, or whatever. The pastor may first wish to talk to the worker or he may offer additional constructive suggestions yet untried. This posture on the pastor's part poses no problem. However, delay or indecisiveness on his part, especially when dismissal evidence is clear-cut, creates an ever increasing problem for you.

• You and the pastor should arrange a conference with the personnel committee to present a history of the situation and your mutual recommendation for dismissal.

• Set the date for dismissal. Invite the chairman or a member of the personnel committee to the meeting. Do not notify the worker in advance of the date. He may become a greater problem by trying to secure the sympathy of other workers and of some church members.

• Arrange to have the worker's check ready on the date set for dismissal. An additional check covering two or more weeks of pay is usually given the dismissed person.

• Arrange for the meeting to be held late in the workday. With little notice, ask the worker to come to your office.

• You are responsible for telling the worker of the dismissal decision. In most cases, after proper remedial action has been taken throughout the work history of the employee, he is not too surprised when told of this decision. After the worker receives the checks, he is terminated at once. Ask him to get together all his personal things before he leaves. By this time the other workers in the offices should be gone for the day.

Should you inform other workers you supervise of the dismissal action?

Explaining the dismissal action to the other workers the following workday may or may not be necessary. They usually know the reason. In some cases, however, you may wish to inform your workers of the action taken to minimize the possibility of distorted grapevine. Some employees may feel threatened by the dismissal of a fellow worker. Be sure your conference with them does not add to their feelings of anxiety about job security.

What are some forced termination "do's and don'ts"?

Do invite the chairman or a member of the personnel committee to be present at the dismissal session.

Do state clearly and briefly the purpose of the meeting.

Do review briefly the history of the employee's work habits leading to the dismissal.

Do remain firm in your decision, even though he pleads for another chance—assuming he has had previous opportunities.

Do be calm and maintain your poise.

Do try to keep the goodwill of the employee.

Do explain the additional severance pay, if any.

Do be extremely careful what you say if the reason for dismissal is based on moral behavior.

Do give the employee an opportunity to talk.

Don't get into an argument.

Don't permit him to bring into the conversation names of other staff workers.

Don't "talk down" to the person.

Don't extend the meeting any longer than necessary.

Dismissal may be the most helpful thing the church can do for the individual. Usually, when a worker fails, the church also has failed to some degree. So, whenever possible, try to change a poor worker into a good worker. This is one of the rewards of good supervision.

3
How to Organize
the Church Staff

What is organization?

An organization is formed whenever two or more people come together to achieve common goals.

Organization is a vehicle made up of definitive functions, related jobs, supportive policies, and procedures to make cooperative action possible.

Organization is a tool established to set up an environment to influence workers in the direction of goal achievement. The only valid reason for organization is output.

What is an organization like?

The three blind men expressed three different concepts in describing an elephant. Their answers were based upon the encounter they had with it. A staff supervisor's concept of an organization depends upon his encounter with it.

One might say, "It's like a heavy weight or burden." This description represents the viewpoint of the supervisor who does not know how to delegate the many details of his work. He does not use available human resources. For him an organization is a heavy burden.

Another staff supervisor describes his encounter, "An organization is like a cloud that comes and goes." To him an organization is an elusive thing, here today, gone tomorrow. He is one who does not know how to use the concept of organization to make it work for him.

Yet another supervisor might say, "An organization is like an empty house." From his viewpoint and experience an organization exists as a framework loosely put together, the foundation and supports not being too important. To him the significant thing is to get something started—anything—regardless of its timeliness or of available resources. Consequently, some projects may flourish for a while and then die, leaving nothing behind but emptiness.

A good organization is not represented by any of these viewpoints. Nor is it an object one can see. One characteristic of a good organization is that it operates so smoothly and efficiently that the staff workers are scarcely aware of its existence.

An organization evolves when objectives are determined and functions defined. Organization involves grouping related activities and setting up lines of authority.

The purpose of organization is to bring order and system into being. It serves to bind people together as they move in the same direction to achieve common goals.

However, organization for the sake of organization does not necessarily guarantee good performance. Peter F. Drucker states: "Good organization by itself does not produce good performance . . . but poor organization makes good performance impossible."

If the church staff is to match good performance with good organization, cooperation and teamwork are required of every worker. Good performance requires living together with mutual respect shown for one another's personality and capabilities. A church staff is a social phenomenon.

What are the types of organization?

There are several types of organization. However, the two basic terms used to describe organizations are centralized and decentralized.

• A centralized organization is one in which all staff authority is centered in the office of the chief administrator. This type of organization is also referred to as the authoritarian approach to leadership. The leader in this approach tends to assume a directive posture in dealing with the staff related to projects, activities, schedules, assignments, problems, policies, procedures, decisions, goals, and so forth.

Some staff supervisors centralize authority in their own areas of assignment.

For example, the directive type person usually sets the goals for the workers whom he supervises. There is little or no participation on the part of the workers. Consequently, the workers are not committed to the achievement of imposed goals. Nothing is quite as boring and demotivating as being asked to achieve goals someone else has established.

As a result, the organizational atmosphere frustrates an employee's initiative and creativity. It discourages cooperation and self-development. The organization itself becomes relatively rigid and unadaptive to church growth changes.

• A decentralized organization is one in which the chief administrator and the staff supervisor delegate responsibility with commensurate authority to those whom they supervise directly. The workers share in establishing the office work-flow policies and procedures. They work within established guidelines in their day-to-day operations. They make decisions related to their work. They work with the pastor or their supervisor in setting mutually acceptable goals.

A decentralized organization results when the pastor's style of management is participative. This approach encourages employee initiative, creativity, cooperation, growth, and achievement.

The pastor serves as a coach during an employee's goal-setting process and subsequent development of supporting action plans. The pastor coordinates the goals of all professional staff members to reduce or eliminate overlap and duplication of effort. See chapter 6 for additional information in writing goals.

In the participative approach, the pastor's posture is one of listening, sharing, guiding, counseling, instructing, inspiring, encouraging, and being supportive in his day-to-day worker relationships. He invites opinions and suggestions. He asks for help in problem-solving and decision-making. See chapter 8 related to the various styles of leadership.

What steps are involved in establishing a church staff organization?

1. Determine the purpose of the church and of the staff. What is the overall reason for your existence as a church? as a staff? Written church objectives give direction in identifying the staff's purpose and functions. See the section "Prepare a Church-Staff Administration Handbook" in chapter 10.

2. Determine the broad staff functions which support and implement the church's statements of purpose. The list of staff functions usually includes pastoral-preaching ministries, program ministries, secretarial and clerical support, food services, equipment opera-

tion, and maintenance.

3. Determine the tasks to be performed in each function. In the secretarial-clerical function, for example, write down every task which must be performed to support the church's work. The list may number fifty items or more. Do not include tasks that church members can and should perform.

4. Group-related tasks to form several jobs (job description) within each function. In a smaller church the wise and economical course may be to combine two or more areas of work in one job description until such time as church growth requires another worker. See chapter 4 for suggestions in writing job descriptions.

5. Assign job descriptions to workers. One of the most important steps in implementing good organization is to communicate job assignments and responsibility clearly and accurately. Your ability to gain worker acceptance is a determining factor in the success of a reorganization undertaking. Mutual respect and confidence must prevail. Usually, the worker is willing to cooperate when he understands that the purpose of good organization is to help him perform his job more efficiently

6. Define levels of supervision and work relationships. Identify levels of supervision. In a smaller church the pastor may be the only supervisor of all the paid workers. As the church staff grows in number and reorganization is studied and implemented, the pastor should share the supervisory responsibilities with one or more professional workers. This is known as delegation. It is sharing authority. By so doing, the pastor activates the organization structure that he and the personnel committee planned.

A pastor may insist on supervising directly every new worker who joins the staff. In time he will find that he not only does not have enough hours in the day to perform his own work, but that he is creating more work and personnel problems for himself and the other staff members. The best solution is for the pastor to set up levels of supervision by grouping related job descriptions. For example, the clerical workers whose jobs are related to record, stenographic, and finance duties (and sometimes the maintenance workers) may be assigned to the minister of education or to the church business administrator. The paid education age-group workers, such as ministers of youth, adult, and children's work, should be assigned to the minister of education; the organist to the minister of music. See Exhibit VI for sample organization charts.

Every church is a different situation and must vary its supervisory assignments accordingly.

How well these steps blend in harmony forecast the quality as well as the quantity of the work the staff will produce.

What are evidences of a good plan of staff organization?

• Provides flexibility and adaptability to meet the changing needs of the church. It not only makes provision for all essential programs and services but also provides for the expansion and addition of programs and services.

• Provides an orderly pattern of working relationships established to make a staff use the church's resources effectively in planning, organizing, conducting, and evaluating its work.

• Makes provision for interchange and communication with inside and outside groups and individuals.

• Assigns each employee only one supervisor to whom to report. Every worker on the staff should report to one supervisor only. Nothing is more frustrating to a worker than not knowing who his supervisor is, unless it is to feel that he has too many of them.

Try this experiment: If as many as ten people are on your staff, ask each one to write the name of his supervisor. The results may cause chagrin. Some may write the name of the chairman of the personnel committee, or the "church"; others the pastor's name (he may or may not be); still others may name two people, including, perhaps, the name of another clerical worker. When incorrect answers are given, it becomes evident that communication efforts have been about as effective as the sign "wet paint."

Each worker must know who his supervisor is, and the supervisor must know that the worker knows. This is a cardinal rule underlying an effective organizational structure.

• Establishes an appropriate span of control of each supervisor. Span of control refers to the number of people supervised by any one person.

To set up supervision lines too thin—one over one over one (pastor over one professional worker over one clerical worker) may be just as undesirable as for the pastor to supervise directly all ten or more workers on a church staff.

When a person supervises more than ten or twelve workers—especially if they represent several different functions such as office-clerical, maintenance, age-group workers, music—he finds himself with no time to perform the professional assignments of his own job. He is spread too thin. As a result, some extremely capable and qualified staff supervisors have been dubbed failures. Instead, they were victims of poor organizational structure.

The solution to an extremely wide span of control is to explore the possibility of creating another level of supervision. For example, the minister of education who directs the work of three custodians, two maids, and one church hostess in addition to four clerical and two age-group workers may decide, after study, that the best approach is to create two new jobs: a maintenance foreman over the custodians and maids, and secretary over the clerical workers. The new jobs might be filled by present workers if they are qualified, thus eliminating the need for an expansion of personnel.

The past and revised organization charts might appear as shown in Chart 1.

There are occasions, however, which require a secretary, for example, to work with two or more people. In such instances, inform the secretary who her principal supervisor is. The purpose is to maintain a balance of work assignments to the secretary, to resolve work problems and to have one person responsible to evaluate the secretary's work performance.

• Eliminates unnecessary overlapping of jobs. Do the job description statements clearly differentiate one job from another? Or will the employees wonder at times who is to do what and when? Each job must be clearly defined.

In one church, the task "operate the duplicating machine" was included as a regular duty on five different job descriptions. The church, in its effort to gain flexibility, created confusion instead. Not only was the duplicating machine frequently out of order and supplies out of stock, but the duplicating room usually looked as if a tornado had passed through.

In another church, the minister of education and the pastor both agreed verbally to make hospital calls. However, they had to hold frequent meetings to determine who was going to visit whom and when.

In still another church an out-of-city guest, who saw several clerical workers in one office area, asked the supervisor what their different jobs were. The supervisor replied, "Well, we all do everything that comes up. We are a great team. Right, girls?" The weak smiles

CHART 1

PAST

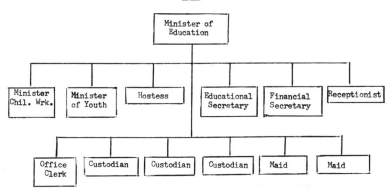

REVISED

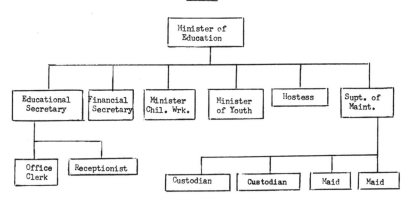

and harried looks on the workers' faces resembled people looking forward to their exit from a stuck elevator.

• Identifies the names and job titles of workers a person supervises.

• Provides a worker with job identity. A copy of the organization chart shows the worker his job position in relationship to his supervisor and his peers. He is identified as a member of the team.

Does a good staff organization guarantee successful work results?

No. A church staff may be well organized and yet not function properly. The crucial factor is the quality of the supervision. A poor organization with poor supervision is intolerable. A good organization with poor supervision is little better. A good organization with good supervision usually gets the job done. Interestingly enough, a good supervisor working in a poor organizational structure may get acceptable performance and production mainly because of his leadership skills.

In time if nothing is done to improve the overall church staff organization, the good supervisor tends to optimize production in his own area by reviewing and rewriting job descriptions and work procedures, or by rearranging facilities to accommodate better work flow. How much better it is for the personnel committee and the pastor to initiate the reorganization project to the end that the entire staff benefits.

When should the staff organization be changed?

• The most obvious time to update the organization structure is when an expansion of personnel is approved.

Suppose, for example, that the combination job title minister of youth-recreation presently exists on a certain church staff. The one job description includes duties in both areas of work. The incumbent is supervised by the minister of education. Suppose further that the church wishes to divide the present job to make two full-time jobs. What preparation should the personnel committee make before a prospective candidate is contacted?

1. Prepare a new job description for each job title. All duties related to the new minister of recreation job (or minister of Christian activities) are pulled out of the present combination job to form the description for the new job. Other duties should be added to both descriptions to give each job depth and scope.

The importance of this step can be best supported by those churches which failed to prepare a new job description prior to the arrival of a new worker. See chapter 4 for suggestions in preparing job descriptions.

2. Update the organization structure to show the position of the two jobs on the chart along with the supervisory and working relationships.

3. Evaluate the new job. Determine by its job description statements, education and experience requirements where the minister of recreation job ranks when compared with other professional positions on your staff.

4. Price the new job. Let's assume both positions rank the same. This means that they are in the same pay grade. They both are worth the same salary whatever that salary may be.

As you recruit and screen candidates for the minister of recreation position, you may discover the salary required to employ a qualified person is more that that which you are presently paying the minister of youth. Before proceeding further, the personnel committee must resolve the salary problem. If a salary exception is made to the new worker, an equal salary exception must be made the peer person already on the staff. See chapter 5 for additional information and helps.

• Another instance that prompts organization change is when a job title is deleted from inventory of staff job titles. There is no work-related problem if the deleted job includes duties no longer needed. However, if some of the duties of the deleted job are still necessary, they should be included in other similar staff jobs. This involves rewriting one or more job descriptions to include the added duties.

The duty or duties added to another job description may not be of such consequence to require its rerating. However, the possibility of rerating a job should be reviewed every time duties are either deleted or added.

• Yet another situation involves the reorganization of all or part of the staff when functions are redefined, tasks are regrouped and job description statements are revised and reassigned.

What restraining influences must be dealt with in staff reorganization?

• The first exists because of the personalities and characteristics of the workers presently on the staff. Through the years one or more positions may have had tasks added from time to time, and the workers now claim "squatter's rights." This attitude often precludes a worker's full cooperation in a restudy and redistribution of work assignments. Also some workers from the very beginning of their tenure develop a strange work philosophy—their job belongs to them, not to the church. Or, perhaps, a marginal worker was employed years ago as a stenographer, when job skills were not considered too important. In the beginning her work may have been acceptable. But with an increased staff and greater demands for output, her lack of skill is now a liability. Consequently, if those in charge of the reorganization study wish to retain her because of tenure of service or some other reason, they must decide either to live with her inefficiency as a steno, or to reassign her to a staff job she can perform.

• The second restraining influence exists because casual work habits have been developed by employees over a period of time. Work production has gradually deteriorated to a "low gear" operation. The workers are accustomed to certain work habits and do not want to be disturbed. These are the workers who, when a work crisis occurs, usually cry for extra help instead of moving into a "pulling gear." Even new workers, who at first were enthusiastic and anxious to produce at their maximum, finally succumb to the "low gear" routine.

Generally, the cause of an easygoing work force is ineffective supervision. Some supervisors are completely oblivious to the problem. They think they are running a "taut ship." Their only standard for comparison is their own work habits.

The church sometimes causes the problem by employing a fulltime person for only half-time work to assist a professional worker. The half-time worker has ample time to socialize, to take extended rest breaks and lunch hours. This situation ultimately affects the work habits and attitudes of others on the staff.

• The third restriction is economic. The reorganization study may reveal the necessity for adding one or more staff workers or the need to upgrade the church's salary program. The question is: Can the church afford the possible salary increase cost? Some churches discover that, even though nominal salary increases have been given year after year, they still have not been sufficient to keep up with rising salaries in the community. This revelation usually comes as a shock.

Conversely, what effect will a restudy and reassignment of job duties have on salary rates in job descriptions? A reorganization study may result in lowering the salary rates in some job descriptions and raising them in others. What effect will such a restudy have on the workers?

Where economic matters are involved, employees may prefer to keep their present job status rather than to risk the unknown, unless they are assured that there will be no salary reduction even though some jobs may be downgraded.

Why prepare a chart of the staff organization?

Although work is performed by people, not by charts, it is helpful to prepare a chart of the approved structure. An organization chart shows levels of supervision and span of control of each supervisor.

The chart also shows the names of all the workers—regular and regular part-time—their job titles, their supervisor, and work relationships.

Date the chart and give each worker a copy. Explain its purpose and use.

Who is responsible for reviewing and/or making changes in the organization structure?

The pastor and the personnel committee work together on this project. The process of reorganization requires an objective attitude. Best results are not attained if one or more committee members allow personal feelings, bias, or prejudice to color decisions and actions.

The workers should be informed of the project. A good time to do this is when they are asked to cooperate in filling in their own job questionnaire forms.

Two suggestions:

• Keep the organization flexible. An organization is never really fixed. Rather, it is both a process and a result. The organization chart is a "still shot" of a changing organization. Organization is not an end in itself. It is a means to an end—an aid to the accomplishment of the church's goals.

• Keep the organization as simple as possible. The purpose of organization is to facilitate, not hamper work performance.

4
How to Prepare
Job Descriptions

Every church has job descriptions of a sort. They may be written, or they may exist only in someone's mind. When unwritten, a staff member may not be sure of his exact responsibilities. New assignments added from time to time may have expanded the job during the years. A real problem occurs when such a worker terminates. Written job descriptions identify responsibilities.

Regardless of size, every church has many and varied tasks that must be performed regularly or periodically. In a smaller church, the pastor may do all the clerical work that is required. Sometimes church members voluntarily perform services such as custodial work, maintenance of the church membership roll, and office work. In a larger church several paid staff workers perform varied tasks. They help plan and direct the education, mission, and music programs. Others answer the telephone, take and transcribe dictation, operate the duplicating machine, type educational records, keep financial records, file correspondence, clean the buildings—to name only a few of the tasks. A partial list of the possible tasks is presented below.

1. Maintain up-to-date mailing lists
2. Take and transcribe dictation
3. Operate addressing machine
4. Operate duplicating machine
5. Cut stencils
6. Type form letters
7. Type organizational record cards
8. Maintain an orderly stock and duplicating room
9. Stuff and seal envelopes
10. Answer the telephone
11. Make telephone calls to people as assigned

12. Maintain petty cash fund
13. Requisition and maintain office supplies
14. Check organization attendance records
15. Edit copy for church bulletin
16. Compile monthly organizational records
17. Figure time cards
18. Order supplies
19. Order literature
20. Book and clear meetings on date book
21. Assist in preparing education budget
22. File general correspondence
23. Maintain file of special promotional programs
24. Enlist teachers for study course
25. Enlist education workers
26. Maintain visitation file
27. Maintain roll of church members
28. Act as office receptionist
29. Play organ for all church services
30. Maintain music files
31. Purchase food, plan meal preparation and service
32. Plan for and promote organizational growth
33. Organize and promote a churchwide visitation program
34. Direct the various choirs and lead congregational singing
35. Supervise the work of others
36. Plan recreational activities
37. Train pianists and choristers
38. Administer church-approved personnel policies
39. Count offering, make deposits
40. Post distribution of budget receipts
41. Compile and type monthly financial reports
42. Post tithes and offerings to individual accounts
43. Mail individual tithe and offering reports
44. Compose and type routine letters
45. Type sermons
46. Make travel reservations
47. Perform general office work
48. Review, open, digest, and distribute mail
49. Sweep, mop, buff, clean, and wax floors
50. Operate heating and cooling equipment

What is a job description?

The term "job description" refers to an organized summary of the duties and responsibilities involved in a position such as pastor, minister of education, minister of music, business administrator, minister of youth, organist, maintenance supervisor, stenographer, secretary, financial secretary, receptionist, records clerk, hostess or director of food services, cook, custodian, and maid.

What forms are used in securing job task information?

Usually, two different forms are used. They are (1) the job questionnaire form for securing detailed job information and (2) the job description form for writing the job description from the detailed information. See Exhibits VII and VIII for suggested forms for secretarial, clerical, and manual workers and Exhibits IX and X for use for staff supervisors and professional staff workers.

What is the purpose of written job descriptions?

Job descriptions serve four main purposes:

• To give an overall concept of the tasks performed in each position
• To show how each job differs from the others
• To identify the job qualifications required to perform each job
• To provide an objective method to determine each job's relative worth when compared to other staff jobs

Job descriptions make it possible to present a great deal of organized, pertinent information about each position quickly and concisely. A more detailed discussion of the uses and value of job descriptions appears later in this chapter.

Who is responsible for initiating the writing of job descriptions?

The pastor and the personnel committee should give leadership to this project. Usually, a subcommittee, composed of one or more members of the personnel committee and one or two members of the church staff, is desirable. The pastor should serve on the committee. His leadership will help to ensure its acceptance by the other staff members and will help to give successful implementation to the project.

The members of the subcommittee are responsible to perform these tasks:

1. Determine the method of securing job task information from the workers. The purpose of the job questionnaire is to get specific facts from each person about his job—what he does and what skills are involved.

These specific facts are secured by one of two methods: (a) requesting each individual to fill in a job questionnaire; or, (b) interviewing the workers individually to get job information.

The first method (a) usually requires less time for the completion of all the questionnaires. When using this method, request each worker to list first the duty which he considers to be most frequently performed, then list the remaining duties in descending order of frequency. Request the employees to fill in the approximate percent of time spent on each task named. Give the workers at least a week to complete their job questionnaires unless job time analysis is requested. See Chart 2.

The second method (b) requires one or more personal interviews with each worker included in the job description survey. The worker's supervisor or a member of the personnel committee may conduct the interview. The interviewer asks the questions listed on the questionnaire, then writes in the worker's answers. The worker's responses may elicit from the interviewer other related and pertinent questions, not on the questionnaire, but helpful in grasping the full content and scope of the job. List only the skills that the job requires, such as typing, shorthand, filing. Do not list a skill that a worker may possess, but which is not required to perform the job.

Either method of securing job information, (a) or (b), is acceptable. However, method (a) has some distinct advantages: the worker, by filling in his own form at a time most convenient to him, does not feel pushed or hurried; there is less chance of omitting important tasks when an employee has opportunity to mull over his work assignments.

The person conducting the interview should be careful not to question the worker's statements of job duties. The purpose of preparing a job questionnaire is to report as accurately as possible each job as it presently exists. Analyzing the questionnaires and comparing duties with other jobs will come later.

2. Prepare the questionnaire and job description forms. Keep them simple. Workers usually lose some of their interest when they have more than two pages of questions to answer.

3. Conduct conferences with the staff members. The pastor should preside and explain the purpose of the project. In a larger church, it may be desirable to have two or three separate meetings; one for professional staff members, such as minister of education, minister of music, minister of youth work; one for the clerical work-

ers, and another for the maintenance workers. The purpose of divided meetings is to give the workers more freedom to ask questions concerning details of the project.

A full and open communication is essential every step along the way to assure the ultimate success of this project.

Keep in mind that anything new or a change that disturbs the present way of doing things threatens most employees.

Distribute copies of the job questionnaire to the workers during the conference. Show how the information requested on the questionnaire is necessary in order to write the final job description. Read aloud each statement on the questionnaire. Give opportunity for questions. Explain the method to be used in securing questionnaire information. See paragraph number 1 above.

4. Request each worker to give the completed questionnaire to his supervisor. He will review them for completeness, clarity, and accuracy. He resolves questions and then forwards the questionnaires to the subcommittee chairman.

This step is important regardless of the method used in securing the information. It provides a check to determine whether the job description statements are correct and if any task has been omitted. Assure each worker that any omitted responsibility that is recalled later will be included in the job description.

5. Analyze carefully the duties listed on the several position questionnaires. Eliminate unnecessary duplication. Check for improper balance of duty assignments. For example, one or more of the higher paid office workers may be spending too much time on routine clerical duties. Another worker who is paid a lesser salary may be performing several tasks requiring higher clerical skills. In such instances, a reassignment of job duties may be necessary.

One word of caution may be appropriate. Occasionally, a worker may make his job appear more important than it really is. The converse may be true also. Every job on the staff is important and needed; the church would not needlessly spend money for salary and employee benefits. Those who analyze the completed questionnaires must weigh each job statement carefully and in context with the statements on all other related jobs.

Sometimes, regardless of the method used in securing job information, the worker is not always certain as to the amount of time normally spent on each task. In such instances another helpful tool, "Job Time Analysis Chart," may be effectively used. See Chart 2 for a suggested "Job Time Analysis" form.

Chart 2

Name_____ Date_____

Time	Duties Performed
8:00 – 8:15	
8:15 – 8:30	
8:30 – 8:45	
8:45 – 9:00	
9:00 – 9:15	
9:15 – 9:30	
9:30 – 9:45	
9:45 – 10:00	
10:00 – 10:15	
10:15 – 10:30	
10:30 – 10:45	
10:45 – 11:00	
11:00 – 11:15	
11:15 – 11:30	
11:30 – 11:45	
4:00 – 4:15	
4:15 – 4:30	

To use this chart, ask each worker to keep an accurate time record of the different tasks performed each day for at least two weeks. Provide a space on the time chart by each fifteen-minute time interval to write in the task or tasks performed.

After two weeks of maintaining the time chart, request each worker to prepare a summary of the total time spent on the various duties and list them according to time totals. Then figure the percentage of each task's time against the total time for all tasks. The results of a two-week job time analysis (eighty hours) by an office worker may resemble the following summary:

Task	Time	Percent
1. Process educational records	20 hrs., 10 min.	25.53
2. Answer the telephone	15 hrs., 15 min.	19.30
3. Take and transcribe dictation	8 hrs., 30 min.	10.76
4. Type copy for duplication	6 hrs., 15 min.	7.91
5. Stuff bulletins for mailing	6 hrs.	7.59
6. Stamping mail	3 hrs., 10 min.	4.01
7. Receive visitors and members	2 hrs., 45 min.	3.48
8. Rest periods	2 hrs., 30 min.	3.16
9. Type church bulletin copy	2 hrs., 10 min.	2.74
10. Receive and distribute mail	2 hrs.	2.53
11. Address envelopes	2 hrs.	2.53
12. Call members for committee meetings	1 hr., 50 min.	2.32
13. Filing	1 hr., 40 min.	2.11
14. Look for custodian	1 hr., 35 min.	2.00
15. Operate duplicating machine	1 hr.	1.27
16. Type form letters to new church members	45 min.	.95
17. Rearrange stock and supplies in duplicating room	35 min.	.73
18. Look for lost articles for members who call in	25 min.	.54
19. Missed bus; late for work	25 min.	.54

Although the faithful maintenance of a job time analysis study may seem tedious, the results make such an effort worthwhile. The chart is helpful to the worker. Guesswork about duties performed is largely eliminated, especially as it pertains to time spent on each of the various duties. For example, it is quite possible for a worker who dislikes to answer the telephone to feel that a large portion of time is spent in this activity. The time chart may show that the telephone is answered only six or eight times a day.

Supported with facts, the worker now is better able to complete the job questionnaire accurately. Also, the recorded day-to-day activities of the several workers may reveal to the personnel committee job inequities, unnecessary work duplication, lost work time, or a need to reassign some of the duties to other persons. For best results, plan the job time analysis during a normal period of operation.

In the process of distinguishing one job from another, two things are accomplished: all information is presented in a meaningful, accurate, and readable fashion, and the organization of statements on every position described is standardized so that all information can be compared easily and quickly.

The following steps are suggested for preparing a job description using the information on the job questionnaire:

• Summarize the duties and responsibilities of each position. Organize data appearing on the job questionnaire into proper relationships. For example, a job questionnaire may include the following separate statements:

File alphabetically all correspondence
Maintain a 4 x 6 visitation prospect file
Maintain a record of prospects visited
Maintain a card index file of members of the educational organizations

Other statements may refer to files, records, or schedules. To include each separate item in a job description summary would be cumbersome. The organization of these four items into one statement may be:

Maintain office files, records, and schedules.

A sample job questionnaire which a church employee completed is shown in Chart 3. The chairman of the personnel committee used the information in Chart 3 to prepare the completed job description as shown in Chart 4.

On Chart 3 the employee listed thirteen regular duties and six others. Note that the word *type* was used in statements 6, 7, 8,

Chart 3

<u>POSITION QUESTIONNAIRE FORM*</u>

_____Church

Present Job Title_____Office Secretary_____Date____June____

Name of Supervisor___Minister of Education____ Prepared by__Mary Brown__

1. PRINCIPAL FUNCTION:

   To be in charge of all church paper and other mailing lists; type cards, letters, etc.; and have charge of the duplicating room.

2. REGULAR DUTIES: (List the major duties that your job normally requires you to perform)

   (1) Cut stencils; duplicate, and mail out "Choir Notes" once a week.
   (2) Cut stencils, duplicate and mail post cards to various groups.
   (3) Make duplicate cards on all new church members for financial, pastor's secretaries.
   (4) Send letter requests to churches for new members (notice of reception).
   (5) Once a month send letters of recommendation to those who request letters from us.
   (6) Type two educational organization enrolment cards for all new members and file them.
   (7) Type record cards for all new members.
   (8) Type report cards for secretaries of the educational organizations.
   (9) Make addressograph plates for new church members. Make plates for all changes of address and other files where names occur. Pull plates of any church member drops.
   (10) Ink all new addressograph plates, fill out state paper additions, drops, and changes of address.
   (11) Make out three copies of visitation slips; one is to be given out on Thursday, one is to be mailed to the department director, and the original copy is to be kept on file. File is kept up to date.
   (12) Mail out church bulletins; perform miscellaneous duplicating work.
   (13) Take dictation and do miscellaneous typing.

3. OTHER DUTIES: (List the duties you perform that are not on a regular basis.)

   (1) Keep duplicating room in order.
   (2) Cut stencils and duplicate materials for educational organizations who request it.
   (3) Order needed materials for this office and duplicating room.
   (4) Stuff church bulletins with inserts monthly.
   (5) Complete quarterly record cards for educational organizations.
   (6) Help count the offerings once or twice a quarter.

   * Original questionnaire as completed by a church office employee

   (Please complete reverse side)

Chart 3

POSITION QUESTIONNAIRE FORM*

(Page 2)

The following questions are intended to clarify the special skills, knowledge, and experience required to fulfil the normal requirements of the job.

4. WHAT KIND OF OFFICE EQUIPMENT DO YOU USE?

(Machine or Equipment)	(Used occasionally, frequently, continuously)
Typewriter	frequently
Duplicating Machine	frequently
Addressograph	frequently

5. WHAT SKILLS DOES THIS JOB REQUIRE? (Such as typing, shorthand, proof-reading, filing, etc.)

Typing, shorthand, filing

6. DOES THIS JOB REQUIRE

(1) Assigning routine work to others?_____no_____
(2) Giving direct supervision to others?_____
List names of those directly supervised, if any_____

7. WHAT DECISIONS DO YOU NORMALLY MAKE IN THIS POSITION WITHOUT GETTING APPROVAL?

(Nature of the Decision)	(Frequency of Occurrence)
ordering office supplies	semimonthly

8. WHAT CONTACTS DO YOU MAKE WITH PEOPLE OUTSIDE THE CHURCH?

(Printers, vendors, etc.)

(People contacted)	(Frequency of Occurrence)
delivery boys	daily
mailman	daily
calling suppliers	semimonthly

9. ADDITIONAL COMMENTS (Which will help to describe your job completely)

10. PLEASE WRITE WHAT YOU CONSIDER IS THE MAIN PURPOSE OF YOUR JOB

*Original questionnaire as completed by a church office employee

Chart 4

POSITION DESCRIPTION FORM*

_____Church

Job Title_____Clerk-typist_____Date_____July____

Supervised by_____Minister of Education_____

Prepared by_____Personnel Committee Chairman_____

Principal Function:

Maintain files, mailing lists, and records; operate duplicating and
addressograph machines; type copy.

Regular Duties:

1. Type and process Church Training enrolment cards, record cards, and
   secretaries' weekly report cards.
2. Type and process cards on all new church members; request and send
   church membership letters.
3. Operate the duplicating machine for all duplicating work; keep duplicating room and supplies in order; cut stencils.
4. Maintain current member addressograph plate file for church bulletins
   and state Baptist paper mailings; make addressograph plates.
5. Maintain visitation prospect file; type up and distribute visitation
   slips as directed.
6. Mail out weekly the church paper.

Other Duties:

1. Order duplicating supplies.
2. Stuff envelopes for mailings.
3. Type copy and reports as assigned.
4. May take and transcribe dictation.
5. Assist as assigned.

Skills and other requirements:

1. Typing, shorthand, and filing.
2. High school education.
3. Experience: helpful but not required.

     *Job description prepared from information given on questionnaire
     in Chart 3.

and 13. In the job description, these four statements were combined into the two statements as shown in paragraphs 1 and 2 of Chart 4. The thirteen statements on the questionnaire were rewritten and combined into six statements on the job description.

Since statement 13 on the questionnaire "take dictation" was not a required regular duty, it was placed under "other duties."

The information on the back side of the questionnaire (see Chart 3) is important also to determine the depth of the job requirements. Question 6, "Does this job require assigning routine work to others or giving direct supervision to others?" often reveals a misunderstanding of the organizational structure. An employee, who really has no supervisory responsibilities, may list the names of one or more workers whom he believes he supervises.

• Summarize skills and other requirements necessary for each job. Note that the job description form in Chart 4 includes a space for listing skills and other requirements. If a job requires taking and transcribing dictation, decide the minimum typing and shorthand speeds acceptable. Establishing minimum skill and other job requirements are extremely important.

• Use language that is terse, direct, and specific. Avoid using general terms such as "handle," "responsible for," or words like "seldom," "occasional," or "frequent." For example, it is difficult to know just what is meant by the statement "handle the mail." Another example of a general statement is "assemble copy for the church bulletin." The word *assemble* is not clear. It may mean "gather copy," or "edit copy," or "type copy," or a combination of two or more of these tasks.

It is essential then that the wording convey one definite meaning and not several possible meanings. The verbs should refer to specific action. For example, use verbs such as "operate," "type," "maintain," "requisition," "compile," "file," "enlist," "compose," "supervise." See the action verbs used in the sample job descriptions near the end of this chapter.

The present tense should be used throughout the job description. There should be a minimum of complicated sentence structure.

• Do not include statements in the job description which are related to dedication, relationship to members, credit rating, and so forth. Hopefully, these values are inherent in every job on a church staff. But they do not belong in job descriptions in written form.

It is important that job descriptions be prepared accurately since they serve as the basis for determining the salary which the church will pay for each job.

Regardless of whether a staff supervisor writes the final position description or members of the personnel committee assist him, the finished description should be checked with the worker for clarity and completeness before the description is officially issued. Especially are discussions with workers necessary if tasks have been added, deleted, changed, or reassigned among the several employees. Your arguments—to attain smoother work flow, to provide for a better balanced work load, to increase efficiency—may or may not be wholeheartedly accepted by all the workers. Their acceptance of change depends not only upon how well you kept them informed during the process of writing job descriptions but also upon your consideration in asking for their suggestions and ideas.

Several sample job descriptions are shown in the Appendix section. These are guides only. Every church should prepare its own descriptions to fit actual duties performed by the workers.

How often should you update job descriptions?

Since jobs change, all descriptions should be reviewed annually. The personnel committee may be assigned this responsibility. When the jobs change and the changes are approved, the descriptions involved may require rewriting.

Whenever an additional staff member is needed, the new job should always be described before the person is placed on the payroll. This may mean a shift of responsibilities among several workers. The new job may fit the description of one already described. If not, a new job description and salary scale should be established.

Who keeps the master file of all job descriptions?

The job descriptions along with the supporting job questionnaire data should be kept either in the pastor's office or in the office of another worker whom the pastor may designate. Copies may be maintained in both offices.

Each staff member should receive a typed copy of his approved job description. This is for the worker's personal use in checking the areas of his work responsibilities.

What uses do job descriptions serve?

Job descriptions not only help the church and the staff workers by defining jobs, but they also provide basic information for promoting harmonious staff worker-church relationships in the following areas:

• They serve as a guide for intelligent interviewing and placement. A person being interviewed for a staff vacancy should be told the duties of the job. A job description serves this purpose. In the selection process it helps in finding a person to fit the position rather than fitting the position to a person. A job description, including its qualifications, usually relieves any pressures to employ a person who is not qualified for the work.

In a church which has no written job descriptions, a newly employed person may be told in general terms what his tasks will be. In actual practice, this means that he must learn through experience what his specific tasks are.

After accepting a job in a church, a new worker becomes disconcerted if he learns that not the half was told him regarding the major areas of his duties. Hardly a week may pass but that he is asked to do a task which was not mentioned in the initial interview.

To avoid such misunderstanding, it is very important to inform the new worker during the interview that, although the job includes definite areas of responsibilities which are named, he will be part of a team and may be asked occasionally to perform other tasks as the need may arise.

• They serve as a guide to the staff worker. It is difficult for a new worker to remember everything told him during the interview concerning the duties and responsibilities of his position. If he receives a copy of his job description, much of his frustration during the first few weeks as a new staff member can be eliminated and his confidence stimulated. The job description is his work guide. He checks himself against it. He talks to the pastor or to his supervisor if a statement of responsibility is not clear to him, or if he does not understand why he performs it.

• They identify workers by position title. The title of the position is determined by the job description statements. For example, a position that has, as a major duty, taking and transcribing dictation may be titled "stenographer" even though other duties, such as performing general office work, maintaining files and supplies, receiving visitors, distributing incoming mail, answering the telephone, may also be included.

But, suppose that the major areas of the position are to maintain office files, records, and schedules, do routine typing, operate the duplicating machine, and that taking and transcribing dictation is only a minor or infrequent duty. In this case, the job might be titled "office clerk" or "clerk-typist" even though both jobs include taking and transcribing dictation. This task in the first example is the principal duty of the job while in the second description it is a minor duty.

In a smaller church, the pastor may have only one person to assist him. The part-time worker may do all the office and clerical work. She may keep the church roll, take and transcribe dictation, answer the telephone, maintain financial records, and may be called upon to help enlist leadership for the educational organizations of the church. The titles "stenographer" or "financial secretary" obviously do not fit. A more descriptive job title would be either "office secretary" or "church secretary."

When the staff is increased from one to two workers, or more, churches sometimes fail to see the importance of identifying the new people as well as present workers by descriptive job titles. Job titles are based upon the content of the job. Obviously, every office worker should not be identified as "secretary."

A partial list of job titles frequently used in churches is as follows:

Pastor	Minister of Youth Work
Associate Pastor	Minister of Children's Work
Assistant to the Pastor	Minister of Recreation
Senior Minister	Minister of Preschool Work
Minister	Church Visitor
Minister of Education	Director of Food Services
Minister of Music	Church Hostess
Church Organist	Pastor's Secretary
Business Administrator	Church Secretary
Staff Coordinator	Music Secretary
Program Director	Educational Secretary
Director of Adult Work	Office Secretary
Director of Youth Work	Financial Secretary
Director of Children's Work	Financial Clerk
Director of Recreation	Posting Clerk
Director of Preschool Work	Stenographer
Minister of Adult Work	Receptionist

Clerk-Typist	Buildings and Grounds Superintendent
Records Clerk	Custodian, Janitor
Typist	Gardener
Office Clerk	Maid
Maintenance Supervisor	Cook

- They reveal unnecessary work duplication. Every office has some work duplication. Some is necessary; some is planned as the best way to perform the work efficiently. Generally, work duplication should be reduced or eliminated.

For example, in one church after a study of job questionnaires, two people in different offices were discovered to be maintaining the complete church roll. Originally, the roll was assigned to one person. However, the second worker who used the church roll only occasionally decided that she needed one also. Any task duplication that is not required for the efficient performance of a job is a waste of time and money.

- They uncover improper balance of duty assignments. Sometimes a person's job comes gradually to include assignments that began as emergencies. Such assignments usually are given to the most cooperative individual on the staff without regard for his regular work. Eventually, these new duties become either a regular part of the position or dangling appendages. As a result, one or more of the highest paid office workers may be spending too much time in routine clerical duties. Conversely, one or more lesser paid workers may be performing highly skilled tasks.

Suppose an office worker in a larger church accumulated the following responsibilities:

a Take and transcribe dictation
b Keep mailing lists up to date
c Operate the duplicating machine
d Type from copy
e Stuff and seal envelopes
f Mail the weekly church bulletin
g File correspondence

Obviously, duty *a* is out of place since the remaining six duties are routine. The six duties are necessary, but they can be performed by a worker who has no stenographic skills.

For another example, suppose a second worker in the same office accumulated through the years the following duties:

a Answer the telephone
b Keep bulletin boards cleared of old posters
c Type form letters
d Receive, open, and distribute mail
e Exercise tact, courtesy, and diplomacy in receiving visitors
f Take and transcribe dictation

Quite evidently, the second worker has two high level clerical responsibilities, *e* and *f*, mixed in with several routine duties. Whenever feasible, the more routine clerical responsibilities should be grouped into one job description and the higher level duties into another. In a smaller church office such groupings may be impractical. However, when a new clerical worker is added to the staff, the pastor or other supervisor or chairman of the personnel committee should be alert to the feasibility of reassigning and regrouping the tasks among the several workers. Otherwise, another high-priced secretary may be unnecessarily employed.

Most church secretarial jobs involve three levels of skills: high skills, such as taking and transcribing dictation, sermons, editing and proofreading materials, typing statistical reports; medium skills, such as typing from copy, filing correspondence and other documents, answering the telephone and receiving visitors, typing form letters; and low skills, such as keeping mailing lists up-to-date, stuffing and sealing envelopes, mailing the weekly church bulletin, operating the addressing machine, maintaining bulletin boards up-to-date, addressing envelopes.

Usually, high skill jobs require at least sixty words per minute typing speed with 90 percent or more accuracy. Medium skill typing requirements are fifty to fifty-five words per minute with 85 percent accuracy. Low skills may involve work requiring no more than thirty-five to forty-five words per minute in typing speed.

The illustration below (A) shows the distribution of job skills included in a certain secretary's work schedule.

—A—

Low	Medium	High

Suppose a new office worker is needed. What job duties would you include in the new job description? Which medium and low skill tasks would you take out of the present secretary's job to assign to the new worker? Of course, the easiest approach is to employ another secretary. And besides, the present secretary has been here twenty years and she would probably raise an awful fuss if even one of her tasks were assigned to a new worker.

Following the easy approach would probably double the salary cost to the church.

A better approach is to incorporate in a new job description several of the medium- and low-skill job tasks presently performed by the secretary. The new description might have the title of office clerk or clerk-typist. This job title does not demand the high salary of the secretary.

The illustrations (B) and (C) below show a better distribution of the skill requirements for each job—the secretary and the new clerk-typist.

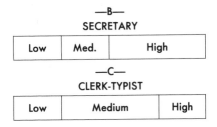

—B—
SECRETARY

Low	Med.	High

—C—
CLERK-TYPIST

Low	Medium	High

Every secretary's job, as well as the clerk-typist's job, includes all three skill levels. Your job, as supervisor, is to maintain control of the distribution of skill requirements through the assignment of appropriate duties to fit the job description.

• They serve as a guide to study salaries of comparable positions in a community. Occasionally, churches may be able to employ individuals without regard to prevailing salaries for comparable jobs. Sooner or later, however, a church finds it necessary to increase salary schedules if it is to employ and hold workers qualified to perform the various jobs. To employ inexperienced or unqualified persons at lower rates to do high-level work is poor economy.

In order to make salary comparisons meaningful, church job descriptions must be comparable to those outside the church. For example, the job title "secretary" does not always refer to the same position in every church or business establishment. In one office, the clerk-typist may be called a secretary; in another, a stenographer may be so designated. It is impossible to make comparable salary studies in the community based only on position titles.

Written job descriptions must be compared.

• They aid in measuring the job performance of the worker. To measure performance objectively involves more than a general, cursory estimate of a person's performance in his position. The job description statements help the supervisor as he talks to an employee about his work performance.

• They serve as a guide for promotion. An important factor in developing staff morale is the placement of a worker in a job which he can perform. As an individual develops, he may be eligible for a more highly rated position when a vacancy occurs. It is much better to promote a qualified person already on the church staff than to recruit a new worker from outside.

In a larger church, a chain reaction may start when a vacancy occurs. For example, the pastor's secretary resigns. A stenographer, working in some other office in the church, is promoted to this position. A stenographic vacancy then exists. In the same office is a typist or clerk who is qualified for promotion to the stenographic job. Now a typist's position is vacant. This vacancy would probably be filled by a person from outside the office. Assuming that the people involved are promotable, the policy of promoting from within is a sound program of personnel administration. It develops good relations, good morale, and usually reduces training costs.

• They aid in a smoother flow of work. Since job descriptions define specific work responsibilities, they help to discover and overcome work-flow bottlenecks. In one church, for example, job questionnaires revealed why church members did not always receive the weekly issue of the church paper by Friday. The individual in charge of typing, duplicating, and mailing was frequently delayed by the one in charge of gathering, editing, and compiling the copy. She, in turn, was delayed because it was most difficult to secure copy from the various professional staff workers earlier than Wednesday afternoon.

As a result, the pastor, with the help and cooperation of the professional staff workers, prepared a revised work-flow procedure and sent a copy to everyone involved.

• They help develop staff morale. Job descriptions are an indication to staff members of the church's interest in them and their work. The first step toward good work organization and coordination is the writing of job descriptions. The worker feels that he is part of a team. He knows what is expected of him. Job descriptions serve as a definition of the church's expectations.

• They make for effective control of job content. A supervisor, who believes that he knows every detail of the work performed by those under his supervision, is surprised when he learns that a certain job is different from that originally assigned or described.

For example, in one church the financial secretary remarked to her supervisor on several occasions that it was impossible to complete her work each day. Occasionally, she worked at nights and on Saturdays in order to maintain the records and compile reports, so the church employed a half-time clerical worker to assist her. Later, a job questionnaire revealed that for several months the financial secretary had been keeping separate bookkeeping records for one of the church educational organizations. This was not part of her assigned job. Somehow, the additional responsibility had been placed on her desk without the supervisor's knowledge.

In another church, a custodian was asked by the various church workers to run so many errands that getting his own work done became impossible. The situation continued for several months. When it was discovered, the custodian was reluctant to return to his old job, stating that he was now a church messenger.

Workers in a church are usually vulnerable to the work requests, even demands, of church leaders. To control this situation it is wise to channel all requests to a specific worker: the minister of education, church business administrator, educational secretary, or some other designated person.

• They form a basis for setting up a formal salary program. A principal reason for preparing job descriptions is to evaluate the relative worth of various jobs in order to assign a dollar value to each. See chapter 5 for information on setting up a church salary program.

• They aid in preparing the church staff organization chart by grouping job titles by functions. The chart shows the names of all paid staff workers, their job titles, their peer and supervisory relationships.

5
How to Establish
a Formal Salary Plan

Someone said that "money may not be everything, but it's way ahead of whatever is in second place." It is foolish to argue that the paycheck is not important. It is.

Its importance is simply that money is a medium of exchange for services performed to provide a person and his family the necessities of life and, hopefully, planned "leftovers" for continuing education, children's education, vacation, investments, and so forth.

When a pastor or other staff worker finds it difficult to make "ends meet" in spite of applying frugality, the situation begins to gnaw on his mind to the possible detriment of his work, the alteration of his emotional behavior, and the increase of incidents of negative responses.

In time, if nothing is done by the church to relieve the situation, the worker either resigns to go to another field of work or succumbs to a status quo attitude.

A staff worker with self-respect cannot remain in such a situation forever. Something has to give.

What plans do churches use to compensate staff workers?

There is no uniform practice among churches of what is fair to pay the pastor, minister of education, minister of music, and other professional and nonprofessional members of a church staff.

Each church has the responsibility to determine its own salary plan. Consequently, there are almost as many varieties of methods of compensation as there are congregations. Generally, the methods used by churches fall into these four plans:

• No salary review is made until the pastor or other staff person, full-time or part-time, resigns to go elsewhere.

• A salary review is made only when the pastor "hints" to a leader of influence in the church that it has been over a year since he and other workers received an increase. (Almost every pastor or other staff worker hates to ask for a raise.)

• An annual salary review is made by a church committee or the deacons at the last minute just prior to presenting the overall church budget to the church for approval. Usually, some committee member pulls a money or percentage figure from the top of his head irrespective of economic changes that occurred during the past twelve months. It's a job to get over as quickly and painlessly as possible.

• An annual salary review is made by the personnel committee. This committee gets facts related to the economic changes which have occurred since the previous review period; has knowledge of the local competitive rates for office and custodial workers; prepares a salary budget including merit increases recommended by the pastor; and presents the report to the budget or finance committee for inclusion in the total church budget for church approval.

In a church staff salary survey, pastors were asked: What suggestions would you make to improve the present salary situation in your church? The following statements represent a cross section of the responses.

"Provide an allowance to keep up the parsonage. I either have to pay for what gets fixed or it doesn't get done."

"Better understanding of the needs of a pastor's family. None of us wants to get rich but it sure does get tiresome worrying about money all the time. People need to know what it actually takes to minister to a community."

"It's a shame when a pastor has to barter for a salary so his family can live."

"The personnel committee should make an annual review of all salaries and benefits and upgrade these on the basis of the cost-of-living index."

"My church gives me a substantial raise each year."

What is a fair salary?

Each church must determine its own answer to this most important question. One thing is certain: churches must begin comparing salaries with the local professional and labor market. Too long personnel committees have compared salaries only with other churches. This approach may provide some value to be sure. However, to omit surveying the salaries paid in the community of positions requiring similar education, experience and training leads some churches, inadvertently perhaps, to continue an inbreeding scale of low salaries.

Your church may be paying even better than a comparable church. But that fact doesn't necessarily mean your church is paying a fair salary.

Another approach to determining a fair salary for the pastor is to consider the median family income in your community.

Then add adjustments for the complexity of the church field determined by the size of the congregation; whether it is a new church, inner city church, mission field, or rural church.

If the pastor's salary falls below community standards, it means that salaries of other staff workers are also unfairly affected.

What are some barriers to fair pay?

A major hardship is imposed on staff workers when churches withhold badly needed salary advances until the church building debt is paid, until mission gifts increase, or until some special project or need is met.

Sometimes salary increases are withheld because of unexpressed dissatisfactions about the work or style of the pastor or other staff persons. This is grossly unfair. Criticisms should be dealt with directly by appropriate committee people. Such an honest approach gives the pastor or other person a chance for understanding and growth. Denying a salary increase should never be used as a disciplinary measure.

"Other income" of the pastor is sometimes considered when the church-elected committee discusses salary increases. The fact is that "other income" (fees for pastoral services, revivals, etc.) is sometimes overrated. And, too, the day is gone when it was customary for the pastor to receive donations, poundings, gifts, and merchandise discounts. However, the church should continue to give the pastor and other staff persons gifts, and so forth, if this is the custom, but let it be an expression of love and appreciation over and above the salary.

Another barrier to fair pay is the failure of the church to reimburse fully the pastor and other workers the cost of their car expense in performing the church's work.

Almost every church has some real or created barrier to fair pay.

Money does make a difference to workers not only for what it can purchase but also to what extent it purports the church's philosophy of fair play.

Also, workers feel more secure in their jobs and evidence less frustration when they know that the church has a salary plan that carries over from year to year.

What is meant by a "salary plan"?

A formal salary plan is written. It is a system that ensures all employees that compensation decisions are made in an equitable and logical manner.

Why the increased interest of churches in a salary plan?

Some personnel committees and other church leaders discovered almost overnight that their church was no longer competitive to attract competent personnel or to retain capable staff workers.

They discovered they could not afford a vacancy. Their salary adjustments in the past had not kept up with the rapidly rising economy.

To meet the economy crises, some churches granted "pressure" salary increases. The increases were not based on a formal salary plan.

In order to secure a qualified person, other churches got themselves into serious staff problems by approving a new worker's salary above that of a peer staff worker already on board. No amount of explaining justifies such action to the present worker. His morale is shaken. Employees are most sensitive to what they consider fair or unfair treatment within their own group.

After experiencing some of these sticky salary and personnel problems, personnel committee members questioned their method of compensation: "There must be a better way." And there is.

What is the purpose of a salary plan?

The purpose is fivefold:

• To provide an integrated and consistent set of principles in administering the salary plan

- To establish internal salary equity—the relative worth of each position on the staff when compared with the others
- To maintain a competitive posture with comparable positions in the community
- To help attract and retain high caliber employees
- To recognize outstanding work performance and reward these persons with appropriate salary action.

What are some practical values of a formal salary plan?

- A budget, or finance, or personnel committee is not placed in the difficult position of making decisions apart from a church-approved salary plan. One question invariably asked by committee members is: what, if anything, should we do about the salary increases next year for the staff workers?

The resultant salary adjustment is usually a blanket merit increase with little or no regard for individual job performance. Sometimes, the committee feels that one of the workers does not deserve a salary adjustment, and increases are withheld from all workers. Occasionally, varying amounts of salary increases are decided, seemingly without rhyme or reason. Cost-of-living increase decisions may be based on conjecture.

A formalized salary plan provides detailed policy information to guide the committee's salary and cost-of-living decisions for the next year's salary budget.

- No worker is overlooked for a salary review. A formal salary plan includes setting up a salary review file card on each worker who is in the plan. See Exhibit XI for a sample salary file card. The file card shows the worker's employment date from which the salary review dates are determined. Past salary adjustments and dates are recorded on the card. The possibility of bypassing a review date becomes remote.
- All workers are treated fairly. A salary plan eliminates the possibility of one or more workers receiving a salary adjustment shortly after they are placed on the payroll or having to wait longer than twelve months.

For example, suppose a church employs worker A in October and, as is its custom, salary adjustments are always effective in January. Suppose further that worker B was employed the previous February. Assuming that both workers were employed at the same base salary, chances are that without a salary plan both workers,

A and B, will, on January 1, receive increases: one after three months on the job and the other after eleven months. Would worker B, employed in February, feel that he was treated fairly? Of course not.

Suppose that the committee, in this example, decides not to give worker A who came to the staff in October an increase because of the shortness of his tenure. This decision seems reasonable. However, the next salary adjustment consideration by the committee will be a year hence. Worker A, then, may wait fifteen months for a salary increase. Would worker A feel that he had been treated fairly? Obviously not.

The success of any salary plan depends upon how consistently the plan is administered from year to year.

• Generally, each worker feels his salary is fair in relation to his job responsibilities when compared to the compensation paid other employees for their specific duties and responsibilities. A good salary plan, diligently applied, is an important tool within the staff's organization and work climate that generates this feeling of fairness, lifts employee morale, and promotes a positive staff spirit that is reflected in the work each performs.

• The church, through its personnel committee, makes a continuing conscientious effort to pay salaries comparable to those paid for similar jobs in the community.

• A formal salary plan provides the base for the church's total compensation package. Other compensation elements such as group insurance, pension benefits, housing allowance, car expense, convention expense, allowance for utilities, books, and subscriptions must also be considered as a part of the competitive climate. It is imperative that base salary levels be realistically established in order to avoid imbalance and distortion.

• A formal salary plan, well-designed, consistently administered, and properly communicated can be an effective tool for attracting, retaining, and motivating employees.

• Intrastaff transfers and promotions are based on a plan. Every job has its description. Every job has its skill requirements. When a vacancy occurs within the staff, another person on the staff who is promotable and qualified should be given priority consideration.

• A salary plan provides the base salary information needed during the screening process when talking to a prospective employee.

Can a church with fewer than five employees benefit from a salary plan?

Yes. The principles of salary administration apply equally well to any size church. The need for a salary plan in a smaller church is just as great as in a church with a multistaff organization. In fact, in the smaller church the welfare of the staff workers is quite often inadvertently overlooked. Usually, no one in the smaller church has been assigned the responsibility to "take care" of the workers' needs. If it's done at all, someone like the chairman of the deacons or the treasurer will, if he thinks about it, bring the salary matter to the attention of other church leaders.

Someone, or a committee, needs to be assigned salary review responsibility regardless of the size of the church staff.

Who establishes the salary plan?

The personnel committee or similar church committee is responsible for establishing a formal salary plan.

The idea of a formal salary plan is sometimes initiated by the pastor or other staff member, a deacon or other church leaders.

What are the steps in establishing a formal salary plan?

An employee's salary is based upon responsibilities (job requirements), competition (what the market pays for a comparable job), and performance (how well the employee is doing on the job).

In order to accomplish the considerations in the above paragraph, the following steps are involved in setting up a formal salary plan. The details of each step are explained later in the chapter.

1. Prepare job descriptions. See chapter 4 for suggestions in preparing written job descriptions.
2. Evaluate the jobs (rank them).
3. Survey community rates for salaries paid comparable staff jobs.
4. Determine the beginning (minimum) salary of each staff job.
5. Determine the percentage range or spread between the minimum and maximum salary. This is a constant percent for all staff jobs.
6. Figure the maximum salary for each staff job.

7. Determine the method of granting merit increase—step plan or percent plan.

8. Establish supporting policies.

9. Prepare needed salary record forms.

10. Determine who on the staff will be responsible for keeping and maintaining salary records.

11. Prepare a staff administration handbook. See chapter 10.

How do you rate job descriptions?

For purposes of this presentation, the job descriptions of the secretarial, clerical, and manual workers are used in illustrating the various steps in establishing for them a formal salary plan. The same principles apply in establishing a salary plan for all professional staff workers, supervisory and nonsupervisory.

All paid workers on a regular or regular part-time basis should be included in the church's formal salary plan.

Descriptions form a basis for determining the relative worth of the several jobs. Keep in mind that *jobs* are rated, *not the workers* who hold the jobs.

Use the ranking method described below to rate the jobs. It is a simple method of interrelating thirty-five, or fewer, different job descriptions. To get the most objective ratings, do not place the names of the workers on the written job descriptions.

To rank the descriptions, select the position description that requires the most skill and ability for successful performance and place it on top of the stack. Next, select the description that requires the least skill and ability and place it on the bottom of the stack. Then, rank the other descriptions between these two. Two or more jobs may rank the same, even though the duties are different.

Suppose there are six different job descriptions to be rated. They are identified as jobs A, B, C, D, E, and F. Suppose further, that members of the personnel (or other) committee are to rank the positions. At the rating session give each member a complete set of the six descriptions. Instruct them in the ranking method. Read and explain the jobs. Ask them to rank the jobs independently without discussion.

After all members of the committee finish ranking the six jobs, discuss the results to reach agreement. One method of helping the group reach a consensus is to draw a chart on the chalkboard,

Chart 5
Chart Showing Individual and Team Ranking
of Each of the Six Jobs

Ranking Team	Job Titles					
	A	B	C	D	E	F
Henry	3	4	1	6	5	2
Carl	3	5	2	6	4	1
Walter	2	5	1	6	4	3
Harvey	3	5	1	6	4	2
Bill	2	5	1	6	4	3
Pastor	2	5	1	6	4	3
Total	15	29	7	36	25	14
Team Ranking	2.5	4.9	1.2	6.0	4.1	2.3

placing the names of the ranking team down the left side and the job names across the top. See Chart 5.

Ask every member to give his ranking of each job while another writes the ratings in the proper boxes on the chart. Agree ahead of time that no one will comment until the exercise is completed. See Chart 5 for a sample of the job rankings for the six descriptions.

Compare the rankings. In the example, everyone agrees that job D ranks sixth, and five members agree that job C ranks first. The next step is to reach agreement as to the rankings of the remaining four jobs. Now, give members an opportunity to ask one another questions about variances in their rankings. Hopefully, the discussion will lead to a consensus.

During the discussion someone may ask for the names of the actual workers in the various jobs. As tactfully as possible, explain that the workers will be identified later when the job ranking process is completed. Chances are the rating team has already mentally matched names with jobs which could thwart ranking objectivity.

Another way to reach general agreement is to total the committee's rankings of each job. See Chart 5. Then divide the total by six to arrive at the team ranking for each job. Usually this exercise reveals rather clearly group consensus. As shown in Chart 5, the committee arrived at the following rankings:

Job	Ranking
C	1
F	2
A	3
E	4
B	5
D	6

It is possible that the group may agree to rate jobs A and F equal since they rank close together in total average points. The purpose of this exercise is to determine through ranking the relative "rank" worth of each job. Placing a price tag on each job comes later.

Why do you need to survey community rates?

The main reason is to answer the question: What salaries should our church pay for the various jobs on the staff in order to maintain a competitive position in the community?

The personnel committee probably will want the staff's salaries to be comparable to those paid in the community for similarly described jobs. There are several ways to get salary information.

One way is to ask other pastors, ministers of education, or business administrators in the city what salaries their churches pay for comparable jobs. Be sure to compare job descriptions. Always be willing to reciprocate salary information.

Certain other sources are usually available. A member of the church, who is a personnel officer in a local business establishment, is usually willing to cooperate. You could check with several businessmen in the church or in the community to determine if a local business firm or a trade association makes an annual salary survey. A local salary survey compiled within the past twelve months is one of the best sources of information on ranges and average rates paid in the community.

Suppose the personnel committee gets salary information on only jobs C, E, and D. Suppose the community monthly rates for job C ranges from $600 to $750, with an average salary of $675; for job E from $500 to $675, with an average salary of $570; and for job D from $400 to $525, with an average of $465. (These are hypothetical salaries.)

How do you determine the minimum or starting salary for each church staff job?

With the above facts, the members of the personnel committee are ready to establish starting rates for these three jobs. Determine first if the church should pay the average rates in the community as the starting rates for the church jobs, or some dollar figure between the bottom of the range and the average rate for each job. Generally, the latter suggestion is more appropriate since it places the starting rates slightly below the average in the community, but in a good competitive position. Suppose the latter policy is acceptable. The starting salaries for three of the six jobs would be as follows:

Job	Rank	Starting Salary
C	1	$660
F	2	
A	3	
E	4	550
B	5	
D	6	450

The next step is to determine the starting salary of the remaining three jobs: F, A, and B. Suppose, in this example, that the committee decides that the total points of jobs F and A are close enough to justify the same starting salary. See Chart 5.

This brings into focus the importance of job ranking which was presented earlier. Since surveys do not always include the going rate of every job on the church staff, the personnel committee must make a salary decision on jobs F, A, and B. The personnel committee uses its best judgment in interpolating the unknown job salaries with the known using the results of the relative "rank" worth of each job.

The established starting salaries for all six jobs might appear as follows:

Job	Rank	Starting Salary
C	1	$660
F	2–3	600
A	2–3	600
E	4	550
B	5	500
D	6	450

Since job C rates $660 and ranks 1, and job E rates $550 and ranks 4, the personnel committee establishes the rates for jobs F and A (which rank between jobs C and E) below $660 but above $550. Job B is rated similarly between the established salaries of jobs D and E.

How do you determine the maximum salary of each job?

After the starting salaries are determined, the next step is to decide the maximum salary for each job.

The purpose of establishing maximum salaries for each job is to provide a restraining salary guideline beyond which the church will not pay unless, of course, a longevity policy permits it.

The salary spread between the minimum (starting) and the maximum (top) salary for each job is usually based upon an agreed percentage. The same percentage is applied to the starting salary of each job included in the study. The percentages used in business generally range from 25 to 50. The pastor and the committee may decide on 25, 30, 35, 40 or some other percent. Suppose the committee selects 35 percent as the desired range between the starting and top salary for each job. The salary spread for the six sample jobs would be as follows:

Job	Starting Salary	Maximum Salary	Salary Spread
C	$660	$891	$231
F	600	810	210
A	600	810	210
E	550	743	193
B	500	675	175
D	450	608	158

Thirty-five percent of $660 (job C) is $231. This figure represents the amount of money—the spread—between the starting rate and the maximum rate of job C. Apply the same percentage to arrive at the dollar spread for the other five jobs.

What are the methods of granting merit increases?

Two of the more commonly used methods are (1) the step increase method and (2) the percent increase method.

The step increase method divides the salary spread (total dollars between the minimum and maximum rates) into 5, 6, 7, or more equal dollar amounts called steps.

The personnel committee decides, for example, that each job's salary spread shown in the schedule above shall be divided into seven merit increase steps.

The salary spread for job C is $231. When $231 is divided by six (the first step is the beginning rate), the value of each step is $38 with $3 remaining. The $3 is added at one dollar each to steps 5, 6, and 7, making the value of these steps $39. The total increase for all six steps adds up to $231.

The complete monthly scale for job C is as follows:

Step 1 (starting rate)	$660	
Step 2 ($660 plus $38)	698	
Step 3 ($698 plus $38)	736	
Step 4 ($736 plus $38)	774	
Step 5 ($774 plus $39)	813	
Step 6 ($813 plus $39)	852	
Step 7 ($852 plus $39)	891 (maximum salary for job C)	

The salary value of each step of the other five jobs F, A, E, B, D is figured in the same way. The complete salary schedule of the six jobs is shown in Chart 6.

The seven steps (including the starting rate) of each job shown in Chart 7 comprise what is called a pay grade. Pay grades are usually identified by number. In Chart 7, job D is in pay grade 1, job B in pay grade 2, and so forth. Two jobs, A and F are in the same pay grade because their base salaries are the same. There are five pay grades among the six jobs.

Several different job titles of equal skill and requirements may be in the same pay grade. In a multiple staff organization with twenty or more employees, the number of pay grades might total 10–15 or more.

Chart 6
Chart Showing Dollar Step Values of Job Titles

Steps	Job Titles					
	D	B	E	A	F	C
1	$450	$500	$550	$600	$600	$660
2	476	529	582	635	635	698
3	502	558	614	670	670	736
4	528	587	646	705	705	774
5	554	616	678	740	740	813
6	581	645	710	775	775	852
7	608	675	743	810	810	891

CHART 7

GRAPH SHOWING JOB TITLES, PAY GRADES, AND DOLLAR VALUE
OF EACH STEP IN STEP METHOD AND PERCENT METHOD

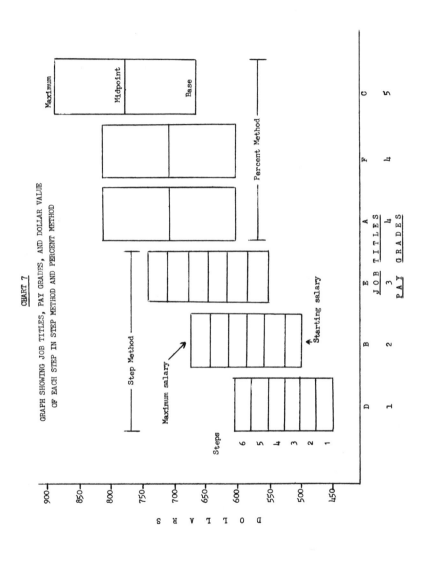

The employee's individual salary record card would show which grade he is in. The master file would show all pay grades, salary steps, names of employees, and their job titles. Additional information related to pay grades appears in the policy section presented later in this chapter.

What are the advantages and disadvantages of the step method of merit increases?

Some of the advantages are:

• Employees know the exact amount of each merit increase since each step increase is fixed. This advantage assumes the personnel committee provides each employee full knowledge of the dollar value of each step in his pay grade.
• The step plan makes for simpler computation in determining salary budget needs for the next year. See Chart 10.

Some of the disadvantages are:

• The plan is inflexible. Sometimes supervisors want to grant a merit increase but not a full step. The resulting decision in some cases is not to give any merit increase.
• The plan poses a problem when promotions are granted. For example, job B's salary is $559 (see Chart 6), and he is considered for promotion to job E. If his salary is pegged at step 2 of job E, it is $582. This is a $24 increase but $8 short of a full step increase. To advance the salary to step 3 of job E is a great deal more than a one step increase. Usually, the person's salary, in the step plan, is advanced to the step in the higher pay grade which represents a salary increase. However, what kind of a personnel problem would you invite if you promoted a person from job D at step 4 ($528) to job B at step 2 ($529)? A suggested solution appears later in this chapter.
• Unless performance measurement guidelines are established for granting merit increases, supervisors tend to grant an annual automatic step increase until the worker reaches the top of his pay grade ladder.

What is the percent method of granting merit increases and how does it work?

In the percent method, pay grades have no fixed increase steps. Instead, merit increases are figured on a percent of a worker's present salary. The personnel committee and the pastor work together in determining from year to year the percent amount of money to make available for merit increases. The percent figure would depend upon the church's ability to finance the plan.

The pay grades show the starting or minimum salary, the midpoint of the range salary, and the maximum salary.

The jobs and salaries shown in Chart 6 would now look like this:

Chart 8
Chart Showing Minimum, Midpoint, and Maximum Salary Values

Jobs	Pay Grades	Minimum Rate	Midpoint Rate	Maximum Rate
D	1	$450	$529	$608
B	2	500	588	675
E	3	550	646	743
A and F	4	600	705	810
C	5	660	776	891

The pay grades of the two methods—step and percent—using job C would look like this:

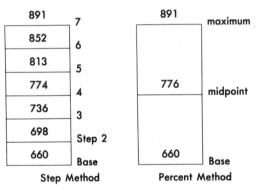

In both methods the midpoint of the range is identified as the control point as it relates to evaluating a worker's job performance. In the step method pay grade above, step 4 is the control point. Salaries up to the midpoint are paid employees who are performing satisfactorily in their work. Employees who are performing above the satisfactory performance level should eventually receive salaries which are above the midpoint. See chapter 6 for suggestions in evaluating a worker's job performance.

What are the advantages and disadvantages of the percent method of granting merit increases?

• The personnel committee, based on available funds, has more latitude in determining the annual percent figures for supervisors to use in granting merit increases. One year the figure may be 7, 8, or 9 percent; another year only 4, 5, or 6 percent. It is possible the budget situation in a certain year would permit only a 2 or 3 percent merit increase.

• The percent method is more flexible for use by the supervisor. For example, suppose the church approved the personnel committee's recommendation to grant a 7 percent maximum merit increase. The staff supervisor, according to policy, has the prerogative to grant varying merit increase percents up to, and including, 7 percent. He cannot go beyond a 7 percent merit increase for any one employee, even though he has funds available in the salary budget of his section.

This limitation is provided as a safeguard to eliminate the possibility of the supervisor granting more than 7 percent to one employee by withholding merit increases from other employees.

• The figuring of merit increases for budget purposes is probably simpler in the step method. See Charts 10 and 11 for a comparison of budget preparation of the two methods.

How do you determine salary review dates?

How often should the salaries of workers be reviewed? every six months? every twelve months? some other plan? The pastor and the committee must make the decision. A common practice is to review the salary of a new worker after six months of continuous employment and annually thereafter. Some business firms review salaries of clerical and maintenance workers more often during the first two years of employment. However, a shortened time schedule enabling the workers to climb the salary ladder in four years or so may cause serious personnel problems. For example: what to do with the employee who has reached the top of his pay grade and now complains he has no further opportunities for merit salary advancement. He would, of course, still be eligible for cost of living increases.

Suppose the pastor and the committee mutually agree on salary review dates of six months for new employees and annually thereafter. In the step plan if a new worker is employed on job E on December 1 at the starting salary rate of $550, he is eligible in June for step 2 with a salary of $582, provided he has met job performance requirements. The month of June, when the worker has attained step 2, is set up as the annual salary review month for this person.

In the percent merit increase method the new worker would be granted an increase in June based on a budgeted percent of his present salary.

The term often used to describe the annual review date of each worker is "pay grade anniversary month." Therefore, unless the worker on job E is promoted to a higher paid job, his pay grade anniversary month is fixed as June.

Unless two workers are employed in the same month, each worker on the paid staff has a different salary review month.

Merit increases are based on both tenure and job performance.

Who is responsible for securing cost-of-living information?

The personnel committee. The information can be secured month by month or by a total of the past twelve months from the Bureau of Labor Statistics.

The personnel committee is responsible for recommending to the budget committee the percent amount of the CPI (Consumer Price Index) increase to be applied to all staff salaries.

How does a cost of living increase affect the salary structure?

In the percent method, the base, midpoint, and maximum rates of all pay grades are increased by the percent amount of the church-approved CPI increase.

Chart 9 shows the resulting CPI increases when 7 percent, for example, is applied to the figures shown in Chart 8.

Chart 9
Chart Showing Salary Structure Change After Applying 7 Percent CPI Increase

Job Title	Pay Grade	Minimum Rate	Midpoint Rate	Maximum Rate
D	1	$482	$566	$651
B	2	535	629	722
E	3	589	692	795
A, F	4	642	754	867
C	5	706	830	953

How does a cost of living decrease affect the salary structure?

The same principle applies to reduce the salaries by a percent figure as when the salaries are increased.

However, slight or short-term CPI reductions may not require salary structure changes. Dramatic CPI decreases or smaller decreases over a period of time may require reduction action.

During an era of a rapidly rising economy or during a depression period a church must have a formal plan in order to maintain salary budget controls.

When should CPI increases be granted?

Usually, churches grant CPI increases at the beginning of a new budget year.

Should all employees be granted the CPI increase?

Churches, almost without exception, grant the CPI increase to every paid staff worker.

Occasionally, however, there may be an employee who is on probation. His work is not acceptable and he is being given a second chance. In such instances, the CPI increase might be withheld until the situation is remedied.

The rationale for withholding the CPI increase is that practically all employees consider any upward money adjustment as an indication of their work approval by the supervisor. Withholding the CPI increase is an unmistakable way of communicating to the employee the importance of his need to improve in his work.

How often should the staff's salaries be compared with community rates?

Once a year is ample for the secretarial, clerical, and maintenance jobs. The salaries of these jobs may change rapidly, especially in an area where a tight labor market exists for certain skills.

Making a salary survey is less time-consuming if only two or three jobs are used in the survey such as secretary, receptionist, custodian. These are jobs most commonly found in the labor market. When you make a salary survey, be sure to compare job descriptions and not job titles.

Usually, the only time a church makes a salary inquiry related to a professional job is when a professional vacancy occurs. The personnel committee soon discovers by checking the salaries and benefits of candidates whether a favorable compensation position exists.

Should the jobs of men and women who hold comparable staff positions be placed in the same pay grade?

Yes. The reason laws related to wage discrimination because of sex came into being was to correct the glaring injustices perpetrated by business organizations.

Churches are in a peculiar position by not having to comply with this law. But, because of explicit Christian concepts of the worth of each person, churches should feel deeply constrained to inspect their own pay scale traditions and immediately eliminate existing pay discrimination because of sex. Why, then, do some spiritually dedicated church leaders feel that a woman in a comparable position to that of a man should be paid less money when both jobs require the same education and experience?

Tradition perhaps. Or that the man is married and has a family to support and the woman is single. Or the woman lives with her parents. Or that her husband has a good job and she doesn't need the money. Or that she's a woman, so there!

Hopefully, Christian businessmen will use their influence to eliminate any salary discrimination practices which exist on the staff of their church.

It is sad when social and government pressures instead of Christian concepts force churches to change their treatment toward committee and dedicated staff employees.

Who starts a merit review action?

The person in the staff office who is in charge of maintaining the employees' individual salary record cards starts the review action. He notifies the supervisor a month in advance of the pay grade anniversary date of each employee he supervises.

Who grants merit increases?

The supervisor of the employee.

In a smaller church this person is the pastor. In a multistaff church this could be one of several persons such as the pastor, program director, minister of education, business administrator, superintendent of maintenance, director of food services, and so forth.

In some churches the pastor and/or the personnel committee reviews the salary recommendations made by staff supervisors. The approval is usually perfunctory.

A better plan is for the personnel to establish administrative guidelines in the form of written policies to permit salary adjustment decisions to flow unhampered without levels of approvals.

Policies provide checks and controls. How well a supervisor administers the salary program becomes a part of his performance review when he is considered for a merit increase.

Suppose, however, the pastor or personnel committee defeats the salary increase recommendation of the supervisor. This decision places the supervisor in a most embarrassing and untenable position, especially if the recommendation was turned down because of some caprice.

The supervisor needs to learn why the recommendation was not approved. He should plead his case. The decision may or may not be altered. Either way the supervisor must inform the employee of the final merit increase decision.

If the salary recommendation is approved, the communication of it is a pleasant assignment. If not approved, the supervisor has a more difficult and delicate communication problem. Especially so, if he feels that the employee's work, cooperation, and spirit are "tops."

What is your role if your merit increase recommendation is not approved?

What should you do besides wish you were somewhere else? Here are some suggestions:

• You should plan what you are going to say to the employee.
• You should not delay arranging a conference with the employee. He is anxious to learn of the decision. If there is too much delay, the staff or church grapevine will already have broken the news to the worker. This situation could make the communication process between the two of you even more sticky.
• You should give the employee the facts if a just cause is the reason for the decision. You may feel the disapproval argument is weak and flimsy. If so, be careful not to create for yourself potential problems "down the road" by leaving no doubt in the mind

of the employee who is the "good guy" and who are the "bad guys."

• You should not mortgage the future by telling the worker of an increase possibility in six months or whatever. The worker may consider your statement as a promise.

• You should not liberate yourself of responsibility by saying to the employee: "There's nothing more I can do." The worker may take this as his cue to bypass you in future similar matters and go directly to the person who makes the decisions.

Shall a new worker always start at the base salary of his pay grade?

Generally, yes. This answer assumes the base rates are competitive with comparable salaries in the labor market. It also assumes the personnel committee has established minimum job requirements (education, experience, skills) for every job on the staff.

For example, if the minimum education requirement for a certain staff job is an undergraduate degree, should the church pay a higher starting salary to a candidate who has a doctor's degree? Of course not. It's like paying a custodian a higher starting salary because he has a business college diploma when the only requirement for the job is to be able to read and write.

Similarly, if the minimum experience requirement for a certain job is five years, should the church pay a higher starting salary because the candidate has fifteen years of experience? Keep in mind that sometimes fifteen years may be one year's experience repeated fifteen times. You have no assurance that one person's fifteen years is worth more than another person's five years.

Exceptions to the church's starting rate policy usually create unpleasant personnel problems. Especially so when a peer person already on the staff and with several year's tenure is paid a lower salary than that of the new worker.

Churches tend to make exceptions when:

• The salary scale is not competitive with the labor market
• The minimum job requirements are not realistic
• The church is going after too high-priced candidates

Should a worker ever receive more than the maximum salary of his pay grade?

Not unless the salary administration policy manual provides for a longevity increase. Requirements for longevity salary consideration usually include items such as number of years of service in the church, quality and quantity of work performed, suggestions which resulted in improved work systems and methods, evidences of self-development plans, and so forth.

A percent of the maximum salary of the worker's pay grade is usually stated as a limitation of the total amount of the longevity salary increase.

In the step plan how do you determine a worker's salary when he is demoted, transferred, or promoted?

• Demotions. Suppose a worker is in job E at step 4 which is $646 a month. (See Chart 6.) Because of lack of ability or other similar reason, the worker is demoted to job B. It may be desirable to write into policy that a demoted worker's salary shall be adjusted to the same step number in the lower pay grade as in the higher pay grade at the time of demotion. In this example, the worker's salary would be reduced from $646 to $587 a month. Or there could be included a policy statement indicating that the demoted worker's salary shall be adjusted to the nearest comparable rate in the lower pay grade. Again, in this example, the worker's salary would be reduced from $646 (step 4) to $645 (step 6 of job B) a month.

The latter policy has to inherent problems: (1) The supposedly demoted worker continues to receive a comparable salary for a lower rated job; and (2) "jumping" his salary from step 4 to step 6 gives him very little opportunity for salary advancement.

• Transfers. Usually, a transfer places a worker in another job with the same pay scale. For example, suppose a worker is in job A at step 4, which is $705 a month. If he is transferred to job F, he would make a lateral move and remain at step 4 salary in the new job. Or the church may wish to write another transfer plan into its policy statement.

• Promotions. Usually a promotion means moving a worker to a higher rated job and with an increase in salary. Look again at Chart 6. Suppose a worker in job E at step 4 salary of $646 is promoted to job A. To what salary step in job A should he be promoted? The committee needs to make the decision in the form of a policy statement which will guide it in this and future actions.

If the promoted worker is to be placed in a salary step equal to or next higher than he is presently receiving, his salary could be adjusted from $646 (step 4 in pay grade of job E) to $670 (step 3 in pay grade of job A). This is a monthly increase of $24. However, the total step increase for job A is $35 (the difference between $635, step 1, and $670, step 3). This means that the promotion worker lacked $11 receiving a full step increase.

This problem could be resolved in several ways.

One is to agree that $24 (in this example) is ample and appropriate and to assume that the salary matter will be corrected at his next pay grade anniversary date. But suppose the increase was only $1 or that his pay grade anniversary date was eleven months away or that his promotion coincided with his pay grade anniversary date.

Another way is to assign the promoted worker a new pay grade anniversary month. His new anniversary date may be figured by using the following formula:

$$\frac{\$24 \text{ (actual increase)}}{\$35 \text{ (total step increase)}} \text{ times } \frac{6 \text{ (six months)}}{} \text{ equals } \frac{144}{35} \text{ or } 4 \text{ (4 months)}$$

His new salary anniversary date is set up for four months hence of the month of actual promotion instead of the usual six months (step 1 to step 2 time elapse). In this example, it is assumed that the policy is to promote a worker from step 1 to step 2 after six month's employment. Substitute the number 12 (12 months) in the formula to figure the pay grade anniversary date of a worker, if your policy is to promote a worker from one step to the next higher in twelve months.

Or, rather than follow the formula method, the church may wish to write into policy that, whenever a worker's increase is less than a full step increase in the higher pay grade, his new anniversary date will automatically be set up six months in advance.

Yet another method is to promote the worker to the salary step in the higher pay grade which includes at least a full step increase. In this example, then, the worker's salary would move from $646 (step 4) to $705 (step 4), a month, which is $24 more than the normal step increase for that pay grade. His pay grade anniversary date would be changed to agree with the month of actual promotion.

In the percent plan, how do you determine a worker's salary when there is a change of status?

• Demotion. When a person is demoted to a lower pay grade, his salary might be reduced to the base of the lower grade or a

6 percent (or whatever) reduction applied to his present salary, whichever is less. In no event should the demoted employee's salary be above the maximum of the lower pay grade. If so, reduce the salary to coincide with the maximum rate. His pay grade anniversary date remains unchanged.

• Transfers. The worker is transferred to another job in the same pay grade at the same salary. His pay grade anniversary date remains unchanged.

• Promotion. When a worker is promoted to a higher pay grade, his salary should be either the base of the new pay grade or be given a six percent (or whatever) increase, whichever is greater. His pay grade anniversary date is changed to coincide with the date of promotion.

How do you prepare salary budgets using the step method of merit increases?

A formal salary plan takes the guesswork out of budgeting pay increases. The supervisor knows:

Every job's pay scale
Every worker's salary step
Every worker's pay grade anniversary date

With these three facts, he can prepare for the personnel, budget, or finance committee a report showing the total amount of pay increase and salary to be budgeted for each worker during the coming year. In a smaller church the pastor and the personnel committee usually prepare the salary budget.

Suppose six workers are in jobs D, B, E, A, F, and C and each worker has a different pay grade anniversary date. To prepare salary information for the budget committee, a salary increase schedule may be prepared as shown in Chart 10. For purposes of this example, January is the beginning date of the budget year.

The schedule shows that $1,326 is the total possible amount of annual salary increase to be budgeted for the six workers. This amount, of course, is in addition to the $3,657 monthly or $43,884 annual salary cost presently paid these six workers.

This example of salary budgeting assumes that no terminations will occur during the next twelve months and that every worker will receive his increase—assumptions which may or may not be valid.

Chart 10

Chart Showing Cost of Employee Salary Increases for the

Next Budget Year (Step Method)

Name	Job Title	Present Monthly Salary	Present Step	Next Step Salary	Amount of Increase	Paygrade Anni. Date	Number of Months	Total Monthly Increase
Brooks	D	476.00	2	502.00	26.00	February	11	286.00
Case	B	558.00	3	587.00	29.00	November	2	58.00
Smith	E	550.00	1	582.00	32.00	January	12	384.00
Jones	A	705.00	4	740.00	35.00	June	7	245.00
Hammond	F	670.00	3	705.00	35.00	April	9	315.00
Steele	C	698.00	2	736.00	38.00	December	1	38.00
Totals		$3657.00						$1,326.00

For example, it is possible that the worker in job B may terminate in March of next year. If so, the replacement's salary is $500 (step 1) a month for six months and then $529 (step 2) for the remaining months of that year. It is also possible that the worker in job A, when reviewed on job performance, may not receive an increase to step 5 in June. The amount of the budgeted salary increase, $245, remains unexpended.

For budgeting purposes, a plan of salary administration has another advantage. The pastor or the personnel committee is able to plan ahead for any needed expansion of staff workers. When a new job is approved, the base salary determined, and the month agreed upon for employment of the worker, the pastor, or the personnel committee is prepared to give accurate salary information to the budget committee.

How do you prepare salary budgets using the percent method of merit increases?

Before you can fully proceed to prepare the salary budget, you must have from the personnel committee the percent figure approved for merit increases. Suppose the figure is 5 percent.

You know:

Every job's pay scale
Every worker's present salary
Every worker's pay grade anniversary date
The merit increase percent

With these facts you can prepare for the personnel committee a report showing the total amount of merit increase for each worker in addition to total salary cost of all employees under your supervision.

See Chart 11 for a detailed computation of the salary report for budgeting purposes.

What are some sample salary policy guidelines?

Each church, through its personnel committee, prepares salary policy guidelines tailored to meet its own needs. Here are several suggested statements:

• Applicants accepted for employment must meet education, experience, and/or skill requirements as established for each job

Chart 11

Chart Showing Cost of Employee Salary Increases for the

Next Budget Year (Percent Method)

Name	Job Title	Present Monthly Salary	5 percent Increase Per Month	Total Monthly Salary	Paygrade Anni. Month	Number of Months	Total Monthly Increase
Brooks	D	476.00	24.00	500.00	February	11	264.00
Case	B	558.00	28.00	586.00	November	2	56.00
Smith	E	550.00	28.00	578.00	January	12	336.00
Jones	A	705.00	35.00	740.00	June	7	245.00
Hammond	F	670.00	34.00	704.00	April	9	306.00
Steele	C	698.00	35.00	733.00	December	1	35.00
Totals		$3657.00	$184.00	$3841.00			$1242.00

description. Educative experience may be substituted for formal education where appropriate.

• New employees shall be employed at the base rate of their assigned pay grade. Any exception shall be approved by the personnel committee.

• The month of the first merit increase shall be established as the pay grade anniversary date.

• All new or reemployed persons shall be reviewed for a merit increase after six months of employment and then annually thereafter.

• All merit increases shall become effective on the first of the month of the employee's pay grade anniversary date.

• No employee shall receive more than one merit increase per year.

• No employee shall receive more than one step increase per year (if the step method is used) or more than 5 percent or whatever (if the percent method is used).

• All merit and salary structure increases (CPI) shall be figured on the employee's present salary.

• Merit increase considerations shall be based on both tenure and job performance. Merit increases are not automatic.

• Each level of supervision shall administer the merit increase plan according to approved budget allocations.

• An employee's salary shall not exceed the maximum rate for his pay grade.

In addition, the policy statements should include guidelines for transferred employees, promoted employees, when a job is rerated, forced termination pay, and wages for part-time and temporary workers.

The salary administration policies should be included in the staff administration handbook. Employees should be given a copy of the salary policies or be permitted to examine the master copy.

Once a salary plan is established, work it; abide by it. A consistent year-by-year administration of a salary plan is an absolute necessity as a support for building a staff into a team.

Strange as it may seem, once employees work under a well-administered formal salary plan and experience its advantages, they are enthusiastic in their support of it and would be most reluctant to return to the "good old days."

6
How to Help Workers Develop on the Job

The twin goals of salary administration are internal equity and productivity. We presented the concept of internal equity in chapter 5.

The productivity goal (work results) is more difficult to achieve, largely because a dollar merit increase does not necessarily gain for the church a dollar increase in productivity. Stating it another way: A merit increase granted an employee today does not necessarily guarantee a continuation of the same level of performance for all the tomorrows to come.

To some extent money does motivate people. Especially, when it satisfies their basic needs of food, clothing, and shelter, followed by security needs such as assurance of continuing income and employment.

Beyond these levels, the employee feels the need of recognition, job achievement, promotion, and challenge. These needs involve his relations with his fellow workers, his supervisor, and how he feels about his own worth. Payments of money to these employees not only continues to contribute to their basic need but also provides opportunity for them to purchase status symbols. It has been repeatedly demonstrated that social and psychological rewards may be much more important than material incentive.

To do a better job, every employee must know what is expected of him, how well he is doing on the job, how he might do it better, and how he can get help when he needs it.

He must also have an understanding of staff organization and relationships, how his job fits into the total work of the staff, and how the staff relates to church members.

Employees are basically goal oriented. Most employees want to succeed on the job. They are motivated by various personal reasons to fulfill their need for job achievement.

Almost everyone has mixed feelings of excitement and anxiety prior to and during the first few months on a new job. This is quite normal and as it should be.

New church staff workers, especially when entering their first church job, are highly motivated. They have high hopes. In their minds they have developed an aura of ideals, work relationships, and work accommodations which they hope they will find on the job.

However, there are a lot of surprises ahead!

Not only for the professional staff worker but for the secretarial, clerical, and manual workers as well.

Some of the possible surprises should be mentioned.

• The secretary who's been there twenty years keeps telling you what you can and can't do in that church. She's somewhat bossy. Should you follow your first impulse, or use your human relations skills to keep open the door of good relationships?

• After two weeks on the job you discover not the half was told you in the interview concerning your job duties. Should you go to the pastor and charge misrepresentation and quit or accept all the jobs they give you, even if it makes you a nervous wreck? Or, should you talk to the pastor about your dilemma and ask him to identify your job priorities?

• When you arrived on the job, you found your assigned office space in a mess left cluttered by the former occupant. The telephone was disconnected. No one planned for your arrival. It made you feel a little sick and disillusioned, not to mention what it did to your pride. Should you tell the pastor you're going to your apartment until the office is cleaned or should you find a custodian and ask him to help you clean the office?

• A week after you arrived on the job the chairman of the personnel committee called to say that instead of placing you immediately in the pension plan, as they had promised in the interview, you would need to wait six months until the start of the new budget year. Should you tell the chairman of the personnel committee what you think of his promises? Or, should you register your disappointment with the pastor and then accept it?

• The pastor keeps "putting you off" when you desire a conference with him. Should you prepare for his review a list of work goals, projects, and activities among which are a few "wild ones" to prompt his immediate desire for a conference? Or, should you enter his office at unscheduled times? Or, should you continue to ask for scheduled conference time?

• You discover after several weeks on the job that two of the other staff workers rarely speak to one another. This kind of relationship is opposed to your idealistic concept of how staff members should behave. Should you ignore their personal vendetta or try to do something constructive to relieve the tense situation?

• You were told during the interview you would supervise the custodians. However, the chairman of the property and space committee has taken upon himself to perform this job. At first you were delighted to be relieved of this task. After several months you discover the complete coordination of your work requires you to supervise the custodians. Should you let matters stand as they are or should you talk to the pastor?

• You discover after a few weeks that the Sunday School organization is not following suggested organization guidelines; is not promoting the weekly workers' meeting or a visitation plan. All in all, the church is just not doing things like the church you came from. Should you begin immediately to make dramatic changes or should you "belong" and bide your time?

• You have been in the church six months and no one has invited you to their home for an evening meal or whatever. Should you consider this as one way people have of saying "we haven't accepted you"? Or, should you consider the positive and genuine friendliness of the people in all your work relationships as the best indicator of how they feel about you?

Hopefully, not all these things happen to any one church staff worker. However, enough does happen to make the examples vividly personal.

How should you act or react? Should you "hang loose?" maintain a sweet spirit? bide your time? Some workers can accept the "less-than-hoped-for" situation, live with it, and become most successful in their fields of specialty. Others have continuing difficulty. They live in a state of frustration. They become soured. They usually quit.

Actually, your responses may vary depending upon the situation, the quality of your supervision, and/or your area of responsibility. The first few weeks are filled with fragile moments. It behooves a staff worker who wishes to get started right to choose carefully his responses and actions to people and nonpeople problems.

Although churches have some common aspects, they have uncommon ones also. The cultural environment, economic levels, church location, tradition, church polity, to name a few, makes each church different and distinctive from others. The common denominator is people and the Christ they worship and serve.

The staff supervisor (pastor, minister of education, church business administrator, etc.) plays a significant role in helping staff workers he supervises to attain their full potential on the job.

The pastor and other staff supervisors must be sensitive to the continuing needs of their workers. They should be acutely aware of how day-to-day relationships affect worker motivation.

How do you motivate workers?

In order for you to be successful as a staff supervisor you must understand yourself, your job, and the employees with whom you work. To be an effective supervisor requires that you get employees to do what you want done because they want to do it.

This requires leadership and motivational abilities.

It is important for you to know your style of leadership. Are you generally paternalistic? or autocratic? or laissez-faire? or participative?

It is important for you to know the way you "come across" in your communications to workers. Are you developmental, controlling, relinquishing, or do you avoid interaction?

It is important for you to know whether your attitude is generally positive or negative. It is important for you to develop the leadership skills such as listening, communicating, conference leading, delegating, and human relations. See chapter 8.

It is also important for you to employ effectively the primary functions of management and supervision: planning the work, organizing the work, directing the work, and evaluating the work. The primary functions of supervision are presented in chapter 7.

The broad areas affecting worker motivation are these:

- The way a new worker is interviewed and employed
- The way a new worker is inducted to the job
- The continuing way a worker is instructed and trained
- The continuing way a worker is treated and encouraged

- The continuing way a worker is helped in self-development
- The continuing of an open line of communication
- The continuing of an acceptable planning process

The personnel committee and/or the staff supervisor may have stumbled through the first two items named above. In spite of their demotivation effects on the worker, the supervisor can recoup by applying diligently, throughout the tenure of the worker, the remaining items listed.

A prime way for the supervisor to utilize and stretch the capabilities of his workers to attain their full potential is to engage them in a cyclical work planning process.

It is a plan whereby the supervisor and professional staff employee establish mutually acceptable work goals, work plans, and so forth, to be achieved by the employee within specified time frames. It is a plan which emphasizes and measures results.

It is not practical to involve secretarial, clerical, and manual workers in the goal setting process. Their work is usually repetitive and sometime initiated on a day-to-day basis by their supervisor as needs arise. These employees are important to the total support work of the staff. Their importance lies in their skills, efficiency, and dedication.

For these workers, job related items which are capable of being "performance review" measured are attendance, punctuality, accuracy of work, quality of work, quantity of work, work habits, and work relationships.

What are some features of the goal setting planning process?

- The plan calls for the supervisor to work with the professional employee in setting work goals.
- The plan calls for the supervisor to review periodically employee work progress and to assist him as necessary to achieve his goals, work plans, and so forth.
- The plan provides an opportunity for the supervisor to learn more about each employee; his abilities, his personal characteristics, and something of his personal goals and ambitions.
- The plan is a tool to reveal areas for employee development.
- A by-product of the plan is to recognize and reward outstanding job performance by appropriate salary action.

Who initiates the goal planning process?

The pastor in conjunction with staff supervisors, if any.

The planning process begins its course with a determination of the results desired. The results desired are stated as goals. The goals may be short-range (to be completed within eighteen months) or long-range (to be completed within two to five years).

What are the steps involved in the planning process?

Goal setting is a proven method of planning the work. The planning process involves these steps engaged in by the professional worker and the supervisor.

• Review the statement of the church's objective(s), if any. All planning should be in harmony with the overall statement of purpose of the church.

• Review your job description. You must have a clear understanding of your total job. Identify your job's major responsibilities. You must know what is expected of you.

• Determine the church's needs that pertain to your area of work. You must be sensitive to the changing needs of church members and of the church as a whole. You plan your work accordingly.

• Prepare a list of projects, activities, proposals, and so forth, that cover the four corners of your job. Be creative. Brainstorm. You may come up with twenty-five or more different work projects and activities.

• Identify the priority needs. Screen the list of items prepared in the previous step. You can't possibly do all of them. So, your job now is to make a considered selection based on the areas of church need and the results they will produce.

When you think of your work in terms of the results you are expected to produce, it becomes easier to separate priority projects from the simply "worth doing" and to separate both from the unimportant.

The number of priority items should not exceed the resources you have available (people, money, materials and facilities, time).

Most of the priority items will probably be short-range. Include also your own personal growth needs. See chapter 7.

Keep in mind the goal setting process probably involves ten or fewer major work projects. In addition, you still have a number of daily and continuing activities to perform.

• Discuss your priority listing of projects and activities with your supervisor for suggestions and approval.

- Draft the approved priority items into goal statements. There are two general kinds of goals: Quantitative and qualitative.

A goal statement meets one or more of the following criteria:

attainable
feasible
clearly stated
flexible
challenging
measurable (figures, percent, etc.)
written

An example of a quantitative goal is: To increase the net enrollment of our Sunday School 15 percent by October 1, 19__.

The goal is clearly stated, flexible, measurable, and written. Whether it is attainable, feasible, and challenging depends on the local situation.

An example of a qualitative goal is: To improve Bible teaching-learning throughout our Sunday School beginning October 1, 19__.

A qualitative goal statement does not usually meet the measureable criterion. It may not meet several of the others named above. Sometimes, however, a qualitative goal is important to include in the overall planning process.

- Prepare strategies and/or action statements for each goal. A strategy statement answers the question: How do I propose to reach this goal? What will have to happen if I attain this goal? A strategy usually accommodates several action statements. In addition to reflecting the goal statement, a strategy should meet one or more of the same criteria as listed above for goal statements.

Some goals may require only one strategy statement while others may require two or more. Sometimes no strategy statement is really required, only action statements. Don't over-burden the planning process by including unnecessary strategy statements just to follow form.

An example of strategy statements related to the goal "To increase the net enrollment of our Sunday School 15 percent by October 1, 19__" might be:

Strategy 1: Promote ACTION by February 1, 19__

Strategy 2: Organize three neighborhood Bible study groups by April 1, 17__.

Strategy 3: Enlist in Sunday School 50 percent of the church members not now enrolled by September 1, 19___.

Strategy 4: (and so forth)

• Prepare action statements. An action statement identifies what is to be done, who is to do it and when it is to be done. Action statements support the strategies to which they belong. Or, they support the goal statements if no strategies exist.

Sample action statements related to the goal and strategy 1 above might be:

Action 1: Write state office or Baptist Sunday School Board for ACTION promotion information by October 1, 19___. (Sunday School director)

Action 2: Inform Sunday School council of the details of ACTION by November 1, 19___. (Sunday School director)

Action 3: Determine the area(s) in our city to be covered by December 1, 19___. (Sunday School council)

Action 4: (and so forth)

A recap of goal 1, strategy 1, and action 1 above should be grouped as follows:

Goal 1: To increase the net enrollment of our Sunday School 15 percent by October 1, 19___

Strategy 1: Promote ACTION by February 1, 19___.

Action 1: Write state office or Baptist Sunday School Board by October 1, 19___. (Sunday School director, or minister of education, or pastor)

Action 2: (and so forth)

Perhaps the greatest threat to the progress of any church is the lack of proper planning. Not only should the professional staff workers engage in a cyclical program of planning but the church council as well. The church council not only is responsible for initiating churchwide goals but also for reviewing and coordinating the planning proposals submitted by the various educational organizations and church committees.

How do you utilize the planning process to aid in measuring employee performance?

The traditional approach to measuring a worker's work performance involved an emphasis on personality traits and shortcomings. The supervisor determined the why and the how in giving direction. He conducted an annual review of performance if inclined to do so. There is a better way.

The performance results approach emphasizes work planning—

goal setting. You become a team member to the employee in establishing mutually acceptable goals, in problem-solving and day-to-day coaching as needed.

The twin objectives of the review process are improved employee performance on the job and a plan for further employee development. You measure results. See Exhibit XII for an idea.

The results approach to planning is based primarily on the face-to-face relationship of the supervisor and the employee. Out of these dialogues plus the supervisor's day-to-day observation of the manner in which the employee goes about his work, how thoroughly he organizes and directs his work, how well he delegates responsibility to others, how effectively he uses leadership skills, and how efficiently he uses available resources provide a vast store of knowledge to evaluate objectively his work performance. The supervisor is responsible for evaluating employee performance based on the results achieved rather than on the effort expended.

You represent an accountability center. You are responsible for work production. The quantity and quality of production is directly related to the general morale of the workers—how they feel about themselves and others in a team relationship.

You make judgments of worker effectiveness. If these are snap judgments, and are made without factual information, they could become the basis for decisions that seriously affect the worker as well as the work. The results approach to planning reduces impulsive judgments. Instead, through mutual interaction involving goal setting and discussion, opinions which are shared by you and the worker form the basis for corrective action and employee development.

Some church staff supervisors have the notion that since all the workers are Christian they automatically have a camaraderie that is mutually supportive. This may be only in the supervisor's mind. The workers, on the other hand, may hopefully long for the day when their supervisor would just discuss with them some of the things they have on their minds.

Other supervisors have a paternalistic or autocratic attitude toward their workers. They give orders and expect them to be obeyed without much regard for the worker's feelings. In this work climate the feelings of the employees may be similar to that of a ten-year-old boy who was traveling with his parents. One day when they stopped for lunch the waitress took the parent's orders first and then asked the boy what he wanted. The mother quickly replied: "Bring him a child's order of roast beef, mashed potatoes, fruit, and a glass of milk."

The waitress, seemingly, failed to hear as she turned to the boy and asked, "Now, what will you have?" The boy promptly replied, "I'd like a hamburger and a chocolate milk shake." As the waitress turned to go, she said, "OK, sonny, that's what it will be."

The mother looked surprised and before she could recover to say anything, the waitress was on her way. As the little boy watched her go into the kitchen, he said, "Gee, Mom, she's wonderful. She thinks I'm a real person."

Why do some supervisors resist the formal planning process?

In spite of the advantages of using a formal planning process, some supervisors prefer not to do so. Here are some of their reasons.

• "My door is always open." Some supervisors feel that periodic employee work review discussions are unnecessary because they talk to their workers every day. They say that they give credit for good work, take corrective measures when necessary, and keep their "door open" at all times. This is good and as it should be. Day-to-day contacts, instructions, and coaching *do* build good relationships. They play a vital part in an employee's acceptance of his supervisor as one for whom he has high respect and to whom he looks for guidance and leadership.

However, even in an acceptable day-to-day coaching situation, workers generally do not know what the supervisor expects of them or what he thinks of their work performance. Also, a worker may have problems that he feels cannot be discussed in casual conversation. He wants to talk with his supervisor but never seems to find a favorable time or the courage to approach him.

Regardless of the kind of discussion, it is sometimes difficult for a worker to be completely candid about his feelings with a supervisor who can influence his salary, his job, and his chances for promotion.

The total picture of supervisor-worker relationships is more than an open-door policy.

• "I don't have the time." Goal setting and goal progress talks *do* take time. Also the pastor, minister of education, and other staff supervisor *do* have important professional duties to perform in addition to their supervisory responsibilities. The heavy professional demands made upon them by church members and others drain their mental and physical energies. Also the "hour glass runs out" too soon and precludes giving adequate consideration for supervisory responsibilities. The situation may be described by imagining the supervisor standing at dead center on a teeter-totter. The plank is balanced, but the moment the supervisor moves toward one side the other side loses weight. This possible imbalance raises the question: how can one perform adequately and efficiently the professional duties of his job and at the same time properly help the staff personnel perform their jobs more efficiently. Some supervisors are so generous with their time that they counsel church members and others to the neglect of their own staff co-workers.

Although goal planning and goal progress talks may not provide all the answers, they do provide one good answer to the staff supervisor's dillema. They *save* time in the long run.

• "I don't need any more problems." Some supervisors dread workers' questions. They feel that work progress talks will open up problem situations that are better left alone—like Pandora's box. Theirs is an attitude of letting "sleeping dogs lie." However, evidence to the contrary is strong. Bad feelings tend to become less strong and hurtful to the overall work situation when they are brought out into the open and discussed frankly. Many terminated workers would be serving on the same staffs today had someone taken the time to discuss with them their work problems and related questions.

• "Everything is running smoothly." This may or may not be true. It may be a hopeful dream. When no immediate urgency exists, supervisors are sometimes lulled into a soft bed of apathy. Then when personnel problems flare, they arise to put out the fire. How much better if supervisors can avoid letting a crisis develop in the work situation.

• "Employee work progress talks are too difficult for me." This resistance is quite natural. Few people ever become competent enough in performance review dialogues that they can say, "I have arrived." But the fact that he is not completely at ease should not deter the supervisor from fulfilling his responsibilities in this area of his work.

Actually, a periodic review of the employee's work goals, planned projects and activities provide a natural base for a friendly and uninhibited dialogue. Goals are being met or they are not. The discussion focuses in on those areas where the employee needs guidance, counsel, and support. The goal may be unrealistic and need to be adjusted.

• "We prepare a calendar of activities a year in advance which takes care of our planning."

Every church should prepare an annual calendar of activities. It is an important tool to provide dated project and activity information to all church members. But preparing a calendar of activities alone is not planning.

Planning encompasses questions and answers related to each dated project such as

How will it be done?
How will it be communicated?
What materials are needed?
How much will it cost?
How many people, if any, need to be enlisted?
When should promotion begin?
What physical facilities are required?
What changes should we incorporate to avoid the pitfalls of the previous years?

Many an excellent calendar of activity item failed in expectations largely because the responsibility assignment was unclear or that the responsible person dillydallied until time became too critical a factor to recover.

How do you implement the process of formal planning?

The pastor proposes the idea in conference with his professional workers.

• Keep the planning process job related. The best procedure in writing work plans and work goals deals directly with the statements of a worker's job description. Be sure that you and each worker is in full agreement about the tasks he is expected to do.

Ask workers to list leadership skills required to perform their jobs effectively and efficiently. They should include those skills in self-improvement goals which would increase their overall work performance.

• Determine the beginning of your planning cycle. Usually, this would coincide with your church year. Begin your goal setting schedule at least three months prior to the beginning of the church year.

The second time around will include some of the same goals and, hopefully, some new goals. The strategies and actions of repeat goals should be examined carefully to eliminate things that did not work. Hopefully, some innovations might be included.

• Plan to schedule goal progress sessions with each worker at least twice a year; quarterly is better.

• During these meetings, progress on past goals is reviewed, solutions for job-related problems are sought for, and new goals, if appropriate, are established.

These sessions are crucial to the successful continuation of the planning process.

• Ask each professional worker to give you, as supervisor, a copy of his goals, strategies, and supporting actions.

How do you conduct the goal progress sessions?

• Plan for the session. Set a date and time which is mutually acceptable—at least a week in advance. Tell the worker the purpose of the meeting.

Review the worker's goals prior to the scheduled meeting time. Make notes or comments. Write questions.

Decide on what you want to accomplish. This may include new goal suggestions for the worker's consideration.

Ask the receptionist or someone to take any calls.

• Conduct the session. If the supervisor makes the progress review session compatible with his day-to-day relationship with the worker, the dialogue will be more natural and productive to both participants. The place to conduct the interview is important. If held in the supervisor's office, his desk should be uncluttered. Arrange the chairs so that the conversation can take place across the shortest desk space. This will move the supervisor from behind his desk to the side. This gesture alone adds greatly to establishing an informal atmosphere for the discussion.

The success of the meeting rests largely with the supervisor's ability to put himself in the worker's place to see and understand things from his point of view.

If the supervisor begins the interview by complimenting the employee's work and telling him what a great guy he is and how indispensible he is (even though with truth), the worker becomes suspicious and wonders when the supervisor is going to "lower the boom" with the critical word *but.*

In evaluating his work, eliminate reference to an isolated incident in which the worker was involved. No one particularly enjoys being reminded of a mistake, or a blunder, or some act of omission which occurred months ago and was never repeated.

Actually, the flow of the dialogue is little or no problem. Both participants have copies of the goals. Both have reviewed them prior to the meeting. The supervisor may begin by asking the worker to review his progress on each goal.

Out of this presentation they talk about why some actions are late, problems which need to be resolved, goals which need to be revised upward or downward, new goals, budgets, and relationships. They also talk about the worker's progress on his self-improvement goals.

The supervisor listens, he gives suggestions, he encourages, he commends as the situation dictates.

Some do's and don'ts during the goal progress review session. Perhaps the following words of caution will be helpful.

• Do let the worker talk; listen while he does so. This helps him understand himself and makes him more receptive to suggestions.

• Do talk about him, not yourself. After all, it is his work under discussion.

• Do talk about specific things, not generalities. Be sure not to become involved in arguing about the meaning of words. This may cause talking in circles or provoke conflict when no conflict actually exists.

• Do observe what he does not say. Sometimes feelings, attitudes, and motives lie hidden beneath a facade of circumventing statements or questions.

• Don't argue. It leads nowhere. The supervisor may feel that he won his point, but the proof lies in the worker's acceptance of it. If the worker becomes defensive, call attention to his reaction without pursuing it further.

• Don't give advice. To say "if I were you" is a conversation stopper. Even if the worker asks for advice, he may not really want it. In such instances, use the nondirective approach by asking, What do you think you should do? If the worker is given advice and accepts it, he may become dependent on the supervisor. If he does not accept it, a barrier may develop.

- Don't display authority. To say, "What you say just isn't so," or, "This is what you are going to do," creates disharmony and antagonism. The supervisor who has to display authority in order to show that he is the "boss" has much to learn in developing human relations skills.

- Don't admonish. The comment "I told you so" or "I tried to tell you and that wouldn't work" produces nothing but employee resentment.

- *Don't use this opportunity to discuss the worker's personality traits.* Usually, a discussion of personal traits alone invites argument and misunderstanding, causes a breach in personal relations, or ends in an impasse. The worker is usually placed in a defensive role. Out of such interviews come little, if any, satisfactory feelings of accomplishment by either the worker or the supervisor. This does not mean that a supervisor should not deal with a personality trait which seriously affects a worker's performance or interpersonal relationships. This kind of problem should be dealt with in a straightforward but helpful manner.

- Don't display anger. Do not let the worker's feelings cause you to show personal anger. Maintain poise regardless.

- Don't pass the buck. "Passing the buck" is blaming others openly, or in a subtly accusing manner, for the status of things. For example, "I tried to get you a new file case, but you know how hard it is to get anything out of the finance committee" or "I did recommend a salary increase for you two months ago, but the 'powers that be' said they'd review it when they had time." Regardless of how true the "buck passing" statements are, the worker feels that these answers are inadequate. He may even feel that to get anything done he must go directly to the proper committee chairman, or another person, to plead his case.

- Don't permit a worker to criticize other staff employees. He may be looking for a scapegoat or be unwilling to face up to his own inadequacies. Although other workers *may* be involved, it is wise to deal honestly and straightforwardly with one worker at a time. A conflict between two workers requires another kind of meeting, not an employee goal progress review.

- Don't close the meeting without mutually reaching work improvement decisions.

How do you help secretarial, clerical, and manual workers develop on the job?

These workers have the same desire for achievement, challenge, recognition, promotion, and acceptance as do the professional workers.

These workers are motivated by the same broad areas presented earlier in this chapter.

The supervisor of secretarial, clerical, and manual workers is responsible for day-to-day coaching plus scheduling a formal performance review session at least twice a year.

Exhibits XIII and XIII A are suggested guides to complete; one for the employee and one for the supervisor.

You schedule a time that is mutually acceptable for you and the worker. Some of the suggestions on previous pages, including "Do's and Don'ts," are applicable for the interview session.

You ask the employee to discuss his/her comments related to the questions suggested in the guide (Exhibit XIII A).

The purpose of the dialogue is for mutual understanding of what is expected and to respond to questions related to "how well am I doing." Problems are discussed and resolved, if possible.

During the session you will want to compare your completed rating chart with that of the employee. See Exhibit XIII. Provide an opportunity to discuss any wide differences of opinion. However, do not attempt to force the resolving of wide differences in the evaluations. If there is mutual give-and-take during the discussion, well and good.

Here again, if the day-to-day coaching has been cordial and helpful, the performance evaluation session should be relaxed, open, and productive.

Every employee on the church staff is important. Every employee should be accorded all the rights and privileges of a staff worker. Your major responsibility as a supervisor is to help each worker develop on the job to attain his full potential.

7
How to Be
a Better Supervisor

In a church with one, two, three, or four workers, the pastor is usually the only staff supervisor. A larger church may have several supervisors in addition to the pastor such as the minister of education, minister of music, business administrator, maintenance foreman. See Exhibit V for sample organization charts.

You are not a supervisor simply because you have people reporting to you. Perhaps you were assigned the responsibility without having been given the accompanying authority. Or you may never have wanted to be a supervisor in the first place, even though you were made one and with full authority.

If you inherited a supervisor's job along with professional assignments, you may feel no particular responsibility to assume the role of supervisor. Do the professional aspects of your job take precedent over other duties? Is your motto: The workers have their jobs and I have mine?

Recall the urbanite who suddenly inherited a farm to which he moved but kept his city job. He did not cultivate the land and later was surprised to see it growing up in weeds and buckbushes. You make a most serious error if you assume a noncommittal, detached attitude toward full acceptance of your supervisory responsibilities. Later, and maybe too late, you discover that you are reaping a crop of discontent, discord, indifference, and general low morale from among the workers.

A hopeful fact is that supervisors are not born supervisors; they are made. Nor does a person become a full-grown supervisor overnight. He may be assigned a supervisor's title and new responsibilities, but he is the same person. The principal difference is that he is suddenly thrust into an environment involving new and varied human relationships.

The situation may be compared to the young husband at the hospital who is told by the nurse that he is now a father. All of a sudden his job title changes. And all of a sudden, he feels a new responsibility. To be the kind of a father he wants to be will now require a lifetime of guidance, patience, and understanding.

To see and accept yourself in the role of supervisor is important, if you expect to fill it. In order to do something, it is first necessary to have a concept of it.

This does not mean that you should spend most of your time directing others, leaving little or no time for the professional aspect of your job. A good supervisor who plans and organizes well, who coordinates various activities, and who delegates responsibilities makes the overall job much easier on himself and on everyone else. Therein lies the secret of good supervision. Consequently, he usually has more time for his professional duties.

Conversely, the church staff supervisor who finds more and more time consumed by supervisory details, and less and less time for professional assignments needs to consider anew how he goes about performing the total requirements of his job. The job may be poorly described, but usually the supervisor is the problem.

Someone has said that people can be placed into three groups: the few who make things happen; the many who watch things happen; and the great majority who have no idea what's happening. The effective supervisor makes things happen. You are delegated authority to direct the work of others and are responsible for their production. You manage things, activities, and situations, but you get the job done through people in an effective and economical manner. As staff supervisor you plan, organize, direct, and evaluate the work of one or more persons; give instruction and direction; analyze, interpret, and evaluate results; guide, counsel, and inspire workers to attain their highest potential. You are their leader.

Another important point to realize is that you do not automatically have the respect and loyalty of those whom you supervise simply because you are the supervisor. Workers may respect the office a person holds without respecting the person.

Clarence Francis, former president and chairman of the Board of General Foods, said of supervision: "You can buy a man's time; you can buy a man's physical presence at a given place; you can even buy a measured number of skilled muscular motions per day, but you cannot buy enthusiasm; you cannot buy loyalty; you cannot buy the devotion of hearts, minds, and souls. You have to earn these things."

Some suggestions may help "to earn these things."

How do you "earn these things"?

Your first and most important consideration is to know and accept what is involved in being the chief administrator of the entire church staff or the supervisor of a portion of it.

• You supervise workers. The effective use of people is still the key to productivity. The way to get better performance from the workers you supervise is to improve the quality of your supervision. You can be guilty of over-supervision as well as under-supervision.

Over-supervision is when you make all the decisions, give all the suggestions, and expect employees to report to you in detail every move they make in promoting their work. You hover over them like a helicopter. Freedom for a worker to operate within his job responsibilities is stifled. Over-supervision encourages employee turnover.

Under-supervision is when you abdicate your responsibility as a supervisor. You relinquish your leadership prerogatives. Your style of leadership fosters permissiveness. Being too democratic may also lead to an evasion of your responsibilities as a supervisor. The result is a disorganized group of employees each going his own way. Teamwork is a lost concept. If you do not know what is going on in your staff, chances are they are under-supervised.

A middle-of-the-road concept of supervision employs a positive posture related to the suggestions which follow in this chapter and in chapter 8.

• You expect good working relationships. Before you can ask your workers to live up to your expectations, you must make certain you are living up to theirs. One way to clarify relationships is to ask yourself: What do I expect of workers and what do they have a right to expect of me?

These are things you should expect from workers:

>To accept responsibility for quality and quantity work performances
>To operate within their budget allocations
>To take proper care of their equipment

To follow established personnel policies and regulations
To be cooperative
To go the second mile when necessary
To continue to grow and develop in their work
To develop leadership skills
To be creative and innovative
To have a good attitude
To help build morale and satisfactory work relationships

These are the things workers expect of you:

To be treated as a dignified human being
To be fair and play no favorites
To give clear and concise orders
To be considerate but firm
To deal with gripes and problems as they arise
To be enthusiastic
To encourage ideas and suggestions
To be informed as to what is going on

• You use the expertise and skills of your workers. You know from your own experience that you must rely on the judgment of others who have special training and/or experience in certain fields of Christian education. You listen, evaluate, and act upon their suggestions and plans in the light of overall church needs and acceptance.

Some supervisors work side by side with an employee for months or years before they discover the employee's full job capabilities.

Sometimes a good idea goes by the wayside because the supervisor is too cautious. Some supervisors automatically respond negatively to a new idea "I'm afraid of it." Other supervisors feel reluctant to accept a new idea because they did not originate it. An idea doesn't care who has it.

• You have a high trust level. One of the most important qualities which builds good people and work relationships day in and day out is a high trust level. To respect others, to believe in them, and to be open with them in all work and social relationships builds trust. Workers sense this relationship. They know when it's genuine. Your example of establishing trust has a way of permeating throughout the staff a deep feeling of mutual respect for one another. This feeling carries over into all church relationships.

• You develop and use leadership skills. Skills such as communications, listening, delegating, and human relations are presented in chapter 8.

• You are available when needed. Nothing is quite as frustrating to a worker as to experience a waiting game until you are ready to help unravel a work deadlock. Being available and being available and ready are two different concepts. It doesn't take long for employees to sense the difference.

Of course, you may need to counsel an employee who frequents your office regarding questions and decisions he himself should make.

• You plan, organize, direct, and evaluate the work. These are the primary functions of supervision. They are considered separately in the pages that follow.

Planning: How do you plan the work?

Planning is a blueprint for action. Planning is the process of thinking before acting. Planning is making the future happen. It is establishing control over results intended. It is a dynamic and continuous process. Planning is more than establishing schedules and calendar dates.

Every church must plan its work to accommodate its purpose for existence.

Several years ago I saw a large unusual billboard in Oklahoma City. On the billboard was a mechanical man riding an old-fashioned high-wheeled mechanical bicycle. The man pedaled and pedaled and the wheels went around. Years later I returned to Oklahoma City and I saw the same mechanical man pedaling away on the same mechanical bicycle. The wheels were still going around, but he hadn't moved an inch in ten years.

There may be some who would take comfort in the fact that he hadn't lost ground either. However, in the Christian context thoughtful staff and church leaders would agree that the purpose of a church is to move forward—not stand still and deteriorate.

As supervisor you are expected to determine the most effective, efficient, and economical way to get the job done within the boundaries of available resources. Then, you must see that it gets done using whatever style of leadership is appropriate at the time.

You must determine the what, why, how, who, where, and when

before you take action. Consulting your workers in areas which affect them is highly recommended.

Practically every staff supervisor would agree that planning is a good thing. Why, then, are a number of supervisors poor planners? Perhaps one or more of the following statements is a partial answer.

• Lack of *time* to plan. This sounds more like an excuse than a reason. Everyone has exactly the same amount of time. Each day's time will be taken up with whatever you feel is most important: routine activities which must be done, making telephone calls, reading papers, rereading the accumulation of mail from the past several weeks, shuffling papers and reports, and, of course, taking care of emergency problems. The routines of each day have a way of usurping the time to defeat early morning resolves to spend some time in planning.

• Lack of *knowledge* of the planning process. Some supervisors shy away from planning because they feel quite inadequate in know-how. These supervisors believe the planning process is composed of numerous abstract principles and theories. This is false. Planning denotes action. Planning takes place when you ask questions such as "what are the church's needs for the next twelve months?" "What resources are available?" "What would have to happen in order to realize successful results of agreed upon goals?" See chapter 6 for further information related to the goal setting planning process.

• Lack of *confidence* in the benefits of planning. Some supervisors feel they could better use the time in actually doing the job than waste time in planning.

What are the benefits of planning?

Proverbs 29:18 says, "Where there is no vision, the people perish." The people lose their vision because the staff leaders as well as church leaders have first lost theirs.

• Planning increases your leadership effectiveness. It involves knowing where you are and where you want to be. It involves knowing how to get there.

• Planning gives you a yardstick to measure accomplishments.

• Planning places you in a position to act rather than react to potential problems or crises situations.

• Planning prompts you to review carefully all four corners of a project to make sure no details are overlooked.

- Planning enables you to make logical rather than "off the cuff" delegation decisions.
- Planning provides more effective programs and services as a result of better supervision.
- Planning builds better morale and creates greater enthusiasm among staff members.
- Planning provides more effective use of available resources.

Some supervisors are known as planners but not as doers. Their plans never get off the drawing board. To plan for the sake of planning is not enough. Talking about what needs to be done is of first importance, but it is only half of planning. *Doing* is the other half.

As a planner, you must show imagination, foresight, and sound judgment in forecasting needs and in setting goals. You must work out the essential strategies and necessary actions to attain the goals. You need to discuss plans with others who are involved and follow through with them. You must evaluate results to discover better ways for subsequent planning.

Some phases of planning may require individual research and design; other phases may best be done as a team effort. Regardless of the method followed, you should, at some step in the planning process, share the plans with the workers who are to help implement them and ask for their suggestions and comments.

For example, a work-flow problem exists. The supervisor privately studies the problem and decides on a rearrangement of the office facilities. He requests the janitors to change the location of several desks and file cases over the weekend. He may be rather proud of himself as he eagerly awaits the workers' happy comments on Monday morning. Instead, their reactions are chilling indeed. They are most unhappy. There is no comment on the improved work flow, but they gripe and complain because they were "left in the dark" in the planning stage. How much better for all concerned if the supervisor had asked for their suggestions! After all, no one knows better the intricate work-flow problems than do the workers. Chances are that the workers could have made suggestions for rearranging the facilities that would have been an improvement upon the supervisor's effort. Better yet, they not only would probably have approved and accepted the change, but also would have cooperated in making the revised setup work.

A good supervisor gives workers an opportunity to use their

judgment, ingenuity, and initiative whenever possible. Suggestions from employees who work with records, files, and machines, or who maintain the buildings often prove to be time and money savers.

It is shocking to realize how much brainpower in the workers goes untapped. When a supervisor reserves all the brain work for himself, he may build up his own importance, but he lessens that of his workers. They want to be a part of the team. Teamwork involves planning. Planning involves participation. How can workers give their best when their best is not challenged?

How well do you plan?

Here is a checklist which will give you a simple, effective way to evaluate your planning.

1. Do you think that the planning activity is worth the time and effort involved? Unless you believe that planning is worthwhile, you will find it difficult to schedule a planning time.

2. Do you know how to write goals? See chapter 6 for suggestions in writing goals.

3. Do you involve members of your staff in the planning process? Get everyone into the act. Let them talk. You may need to subordinate some of your personal ideas or views and accept the consensus of the group. Oftentimes, the group will come up with a superior plan. Remember that people want to be involved if the activity affects them. When people are involved in planning, they are usually willing to accept assignments to make the plans work.

4. Do you periodically set aside a time for planning? Determine your best time for planning. The length of planning time varies, depending on the goals to be initiated and/or the goals to be reached.

5. Do you demonstrate good planning practices to the workers? The good planning example of the supervisor usually begets good planning by others.

Organizing: How do you organize the work?

There is a difference between the staff organization and organizing the work of the staff.

Organization refers to identifying the functions of a church staff such as pastoral ministries, education ministries, office and clerical support, food services, and maintenance. Each function is broken down into several related job descriptions. The organization chart emerges showing relationships. See chapter 3 for additional information of staff organization.

Organizing the work refers to the grouping and arranging of your available resources in order to accomplish your goals and work plans effectively and economically.

At times you will need to change your original goal plans because of inadequate resources or because the need no longer exists. Organizing involves planning and planning involves organizing. Organizing the work may involve enlisting and training volunteer workers for a certain project.

A positive attitude toward organizing the work usually begins at your own desk. An effective utilization of this primary function of supervision helps you to get on top of your job and stay there.

You set a good example. Your office, desk, files, and dictation are well organized. You organize the professional as well as the supervisory aspects of your job. This does not mean you "worship" efficiency. Rather, you recognize that greater efficiency in getting the job done emerges from setting up proper and adequate schedules, work flow, work procedures, and so forth.

Here are some problem indicators, if you have difficulty in getting on top of your work.

> Do you put things off?
> Do you wait several weeks to answer correspondence?
> Do you depend on mental rather than written notes?
> Do you work piecemeal?
> Do you usually perform the easier jobs first?
> Do you overplan?
> Do you build up a job's difficulty beforehand?
> Do you perform tasks which should be delegated?
> Do you tend to over-socialize?
> Do you call lots of meetings?

Usually, the person who is on top of his job is more fit to live with.

Directing: What is involved in directing the work?

The directing is the "do" part of your job. It involves such continuing tasks as coaching, counseling, leading, directing, guiding, training, informing, explaining, instructing, motivating, and inspiriting.

Directing the work involves the three "P's": people, programs, and problems. And you can't have one without at least one of the others.

Directing the work involves the use of leadership skills. Getting the job done is not a question of having power over a worker but having influence with him.

The quality of the acceptance of your direction by workers is directly related to how well they feel you are living up to their expectations in all work relationships.

Directing the work includes these supervisory responsibilities:

• You coordinate the work. You adjust, adapt, and synchronize the efforts of your group to meet work schedules, deadlines, and goals. Coordination takes place when you bring workers, materials, and equipment together to accomplish desired work goals. Lack of coordination causes one to be like the proverbial man who got on his horse and rode off in all directions. Coordination is a continuous activity.

• You assign tasks. Each person reporting to you must understand his work assignment and how to perform it. He should also understand the degree of supervision—close or general—he will receive on all or certain project assignments.

• You communicate. You inform your workers when there are changes in policy, work procedures, work flow, and schedules. You explain changes in employee benefits, personnel policies, and in organization structure. You set up formal discussions with professional workers and discuss their progress in reaching goals. You schedule conferences with workers for the purpose of giving information, solving problems, sharing ideas, and so forth.

• You make decisions in keeping with your assigned authority. You may wish to consult first with those who would be affected by the decision or make the decision unilaterally. The method you use depends largely on the situation and whether it's a major or minor decision. A good supervisor is decisive.

• You improve work methods. You should be constantly alert to discovering better methods for doing the work. You should encourage your workers to make suggestions for work improvement systems. Sometimes the simple relocation of a desk or a file cabinet not only increases efficiency but also reduces fatigue.

- You establish controls to assure achievement of approved goals, projects, activities and so forth. It is a system for comparing actual results with planned results. Control means to guide a goal, project, or activity in the direction intended.

For example, you control when you examine, investigate, and evaluate the progress of a project against predetermined time schedules. You check to see if everything is in order. If not, there may still be time to take whatever action is necessary to correct the unsatisfactory progress of the work plan.

Any supervisor, who waits until deadline dates before he examines the progress of a project, may find that he is in a most embarrassing position. He may censure the workers assigned to the project as a way of releasing his personal feelings. A supervisor demonstrates maturity when he reacts quickly to a crisis and takes positive remedial action. His maturity may be questioned, however, if he lives from one crisis to another. Some supervisors soon learn that periodical checking on the progress of various projects and activities is far better than pampering ulcers.

Sometimes the supervisor may assign responsibility for checking the progress of an activity to another staff worker. If this person is so instructed, he makes the necessary reports, verbal or written, and takes corrective actions when unsatisfactory conditions occur.

One obvious control is the financial budget. The supervisor should study the monthly or quarterly financial reports carefully to ascertain his actual expenditures against those budgeted. The financial statement also reveals unexpended budgeted funds which serve as a guide as well as a control for future activities and their costs.

Other controls are dated deadlines, procedures, established goals, and reports.

- You develop the workers you supervise. You discover training needs through observation and through the process of setting mutually acceptable goals. You work with each employee in deciding what training opportunities are available locally such as workshops, seminars, or night classes. The city library is another resource. See chapter 6 on writing goals.

- You lead and inspirit employees to do their best work.

Some supervisors believe that money and things are the worker's highest motivators. To say that an employee is not influenced by the check in his pay envelope is foolish. However, money alone does not motivate an employee to do his best. In fact, the supervisor who measures a worker's loyalty, cooperation, and dedication solely in terms of salary can never pay enough money.

Through personnel research industry has found that employees place several "wants" ahead of wages. Some of these are job security, job satisfaction, recognition, good supervision, and promotion.

For most individuals, the greater satisfaction and strongest motivation are derived from achievement, responsibility, growth, earned recognition, and work itself. When an employee is motivated by these, he is happily identified with his job.

Supervision, then, plays a significant role in the proper work motivation of an employee. One big job of a supervisor is to know why people act as they do. Knowing a worker's motives and goals helps him to understand the *why* of the worker's behavior.

People vary greatly in their likes, dislikes, personality makeup, life's goals, and so forth. Since people are very complex, the wise supervisor deals with them as individuals. Usually, when workers cooperate and perform as a superb team, the underlying explanation lies in the supervisor's skill and ability to treat them as important individuals. A good supervisor does not push people down; he lifts them up.

An effective supervisor provides each new worker with job information and plans carefully his overall job orientation. For all workers, the supervisor provides incentives for maintaining high performance, encourages the exercise of independent judgment, fosters and invites ideas for better ways to perform the work, gives recognition for work well-done, and creates a participative climate in which the worker knows he is expected to learn from his own mistakes. The supervisor is the key person in the motivation process.

Evaluating: How well do you evaluate the work?

The cycle of planning, organizing, and directing the work is not complete until the work is evaluated. Evaluation is probably one of the most important functions of a supervisor. Yet, it seems to be the most neglected.

Usually, whenever a project or activity is over it seems that almost everyone is glad. Everyone involved has worked hard. It has taken a lot of time and energy. "Let's forget the whole thing until next year" is the unspoken consensus.

However, it rarely fails that when next year arrives to plan a similar project, such as a Vacation Bible School, a flurry of questions are asked about the past year's effort. And either no one knows or there are conflicting reports.

How much better it would be to evaluate the results before putting the project to bed.

You evaluate, periodically, the appropriateness of goals, strategies, and supporting actions in your assigned area of work. You evaluate the work of employees you supervise and counsel with them on ways to improve in their work.

You evaluate systems, work flow, and procedures periodically.

You also evaluate completed goals, projects, and activities by asking your workers and others to respond to questions such as:

- What was the purpose of the goal or project?
- Did we reach the goal?
- What were the tangible results?
- How could we have accomplished even more acceptable results?
- Was the timing right? Why?
- Did we over or under promote? In what way?
- Would you alter the planning phase? Why?
- How could we have improved our communication of the goal or project?
- Did we adequaely use our resources? (people, money, time, facilities, and equipment)
- Did we coordinate the activity with the church calendar?
- Should we include the goal or project in next year's plans? Why?
- What feedback did we hear from church members?
- What could the supervisor-director have done to enhance the success of this effort?

The evaluation meeting should be scheduled within a week or two after a project is completed. Otherwise, many of the benefits of a full appraisal are lost.

Before the evaluation meeting ask someone to take notes on responses at the evaluation meeting.

Encourage openness in expressing positive and negative feelings. Without forcing the approach, strive to get participation from all council members.

Place the notes of the evaluation meeting in a folder for future reference. The details of the evaluation, when recorded, come to life when the same or similar goal or project surfaces in the future. Conserve experience, time, and effort by using evaluation records.

The four primary functions of supervision named above—planning, organizing, directing, and evaluating—comprise the main part of your work. From them several of your job description statements emerge.

The word *plan* in a job description statement tells the supervisor that he *is* to plan, but it does not tell him *how* to plan. His success in carrying out the intent of the duty depends upon the degree of skill he demonstrates in the "planning process." In this context, "plan" is not a trite action verb prefixed to a duty statement, but it becomes the central force around which the duty takes on significant meaning and purpose.

The answer to the question, "How proficient are you in planning, or in organizing, or in motivating?" obviously lies in the effective results produced through the use of these functions.

The supervisor is the most important person in the work life of those whom he supervises. Supervision is not a lazy man's job.

How you can become a better supervisor?

"Well, did you learn anything today?" the teenager asked, as her six-year-old brother sauntered in from his first day at school.

"No, not much," he replied, as he continued his way to the refrigerator. "Guess I'll have to go back tomorrow."

What a profound answer! Not only tomorrow, but many tomorrows—as long as he lives—he will be in some sort of school.

The only difference that time makes is the change from education as such, which is ordinarily quite broad in scope, to one or more specific training and improvement objectives related directly to the job.

Persons in almost all fields of professional activity must continue to study beyond their formal education if they are to keep pace with changing concepts, improved methods, and applications. The church-paid staff supervisor is no exception.

The man who, upon graduation, says to himself, "I finally made it; now I can rest awhile," is like the person who rows to the midde of a placid lake and then pulls in his oars. Although the impetus of years of formal training may carry a person forward for a time, he soon becomes aware that he must reactivate the oars of study to move forward—even to maintain—his position as a leader.

The statement of a baseball player, Satchel Paige, "Never look back; something may be gaining on you," may be appropriate advice. The forward look is important to the fulfillment of a person's life purposes.

The better trained a person is the more productive he can be. This does not necessarily mean that a well-trained person *will* be more productive, but it does mean that he *can* be more productive. His "drive" factors depend largely upon how much incentive his job furnishes for the achievement at top performance.

Every man's self-development is an individual matter. The best laboratory is the job itself where a man's development is largely the result of his day-to-day work experiences. This does not mean that putting in the hours over a period of time will automatically develop a supervisor into a full-blown leader in his field. When ten years have passed, he may find that all he has had is one year of experience repeated ten times.

How can you grow and develop on the job? The following suggestions may be helpful:

• Analyze your job duties. What are your responsibilities? Write them down. Some supervisors may say, "I know what I'm supposed to do. Why do I need to write job statements?" There are several reasons:

To make certain that all the duties of the job are receiving proportionate attention and emphasis. Otherwise, you may tend to perform only in those areas which you most enjoy and to avoid those you do not like.

To check the job duties with your supervisor and to reach full agreement as to the accuracy of the statements. Agreement helps to avoid future uncomfortable moments of interpersonal misunderstanding.

Use the following as a basis for a plan of self-development.

• Analyze the skills required by your job description. Although your main job is to plan, organize, direct, and evaluate the work, a careful study of your job statements reveals the leadership skills required for successful performance.

For example, the supervisor's impact of leadership upon the thoughts and actions of others expresses itself through his ability to write to individuals; speak to groups; lead conferences; organize groups; plan programs; set up schedules of activities and work flow; enlist and train workers; delegate responsibilities; to listen; visit members and prospects; conduct staff meetings; interview applicants; coordinate activities; plan and control budgets; evaluate results—to name a few.

You should rate yourself in each of the above actions (and others) by using the following evaluations:

My strongest point
Fairly skilled in this one
I need to work on this one
I really need to work on this one
May be the cause of some of my problems

See chapter 8 for further information related to developing leadership skills.

• Select two or three of the major job skills in the description in which you need improvement. For example, more effectiveness in leading conferences. How could a program of improvement be planned? What items would be included? What sort of a time schedule could be set up? How could actual skill improvement in leading conferences be evaluated? See chapter 9.

The improvement plan might include reading several books on conference leading and attending a seminar or workshop on the subject. After even casual study, improvement in subsequent conference leadership is often revealed. Give close attention to conference room mannerisms, behavior, and habits which negate best results. Sometimes, in spite of all resolves beforehand, and conscious efforts during the conference itself, some hopefully shelved habits reappear during the proceedings. Don't despair. Try again. This is important to self-development.

Everyone needs to increase his effectiveness in one or more job leadership skills. Effectiveness can be acquired first, by a recognition of the need, second, by a desire to improve, and third, by doing something about it. Generally, a poor application of leadership skills makes a supervisor-professional worker ineffective on his job—not a lack of his professional ability.

However, attending conferences, workshops, and so forth indiscriminately for the sake of accumulating hours is not efficient self-development planning. Learning by trial and error alone is usually a waste of time. Rather, a self-development program should be planned, scheduled, and carried out systematically.

Self-development, then, is best learned through a direct application of knowledge and skills to the requirements of the job.

Since you cannot create more hours in the day, your only choice is to order these hours so as to be more effective in fulfilling the demands of your work.

In the process you can become a better supervisor-leader.

Can the primary functions of supervision be adapted for use by the nonsupervisor?

Yes. The nonsupervisor professional staff worker such as minister of youth, minister of childrens' work, minister of Christian activities, and so forth engages in the same work process functions as the supervisor. He plans, organizes, directs, and evaluates. The difference is that the nonsupervisor relates these functions to his own work assignment and as they relate to volunteer workers, rather than through the work of staff employees.

Your work process would follow these steps:

• Planning your work. This is the preparation phase. You determine your goals, projects, and activities. You get the facts. You consult with your staff supervisor as well as schedule planning meetings with appropriate volunteer workers. You decide on courses of action.

• Organizing your work. You put together your plan of action. You decide what will be done, when it will be done, and who will do it. Review carefully your available resources (people, money, materials, facilities, equipment, and time).

• Directing or leading the work. You coordinate the various facets of a project. You assign tasks to volunteer workers. You communicate your plans to those you wish to reach. You establish controls to assure achievement of your goals, projects, and activities. You motivate volunteer workers.

• Evaluating your work. Evaluation should take place immediately after the conclusion of a project or activity. The value of a written evaluation is for review during the next planning cycle.

8
How to Develop
Leadership Skills

Continuing staff work marked by progress is not self-generated. One or more persons are responsible to keep the work moving forward. They are the leaders. Sometimes it is a supervisor who gives thrust to achieving. At other times it may be a professional worker or a secretary. They are all on the same team and harmonize their efforts to the common goal and good of the staff and the church.

The quality of the results of a goal or project depends largely on the effective use of leadership skills during the planning, organizing, and directing stages. The material on the following pages can be adapted for use by both the supervisor and the nonsupervisor.

What is leadership?

Leadership is the activity of influencing workers to cooperate in work plans, projects, and goals which they come to find desirable.

Leadership is not identified so much with position or status or authority as it is with the quality of relationships that exist from day-to-day and the interaction that takes place between and among workers.

Leadership is more than an interlude showing up only when emergencies arise. Leadership is a continuous effort.

Your workers can help make you the leader you want to be. You become their leader when they allow you to influence their thinking and their behavior.

If you are to be a successful leader, your day-to-day interactions with your workers and your attitude towards them must involve reinforcement of their acceptance of you through your satisfying their expectations of you.

The late Vince Lombardi once remarked, "Coaches who can outline plays on the chalkboard are a dime a dozen. The ones who succeed are those who can get inside their players and motivate them."

When staff workers are not motivated to the achievement of goals, each will tend to fashion his own job according to his likes and pleasures.

Church staffs which have a high achievement motive have leaders who have welded a group of workers into a cohesive team.

Employees, as well as church leaders, want competent staff leadership.

What do church leaders expect of you as a leader on the church staff?

It is extremely important for the church staff leader to understand the expectations of church lay leaders. Expectations vary according to:

Whether you are the first person in your field of work to come to the church staff;

Whether the previous person left under pleasant or unpleasant circumstances;

The notions or concepts lay leaders have of your work assignments;

The degree of openness lay leaders have in accepting change and new ideas.

Generally, church leaders expect you to have the expertise to show them how to get the job done rather than do it all yourself.

Specifically, church leaders expect you:

1. To demonstrate the use of leadership skills such as communication, listening, leading conferences, delegating, and human relations, etc. Lay leaders may not have identified these skills as such, but they are acutely aware of them when they are poorly used.

2. To plan, organize, direct, and evaluate the work assigned you. See chapter 7.

3. To effectively use administrative tools such as budgets, policies, procedures, forms, and reports.

4. To effectively use the church's resources of people, money, facilities, equipment, and time.

What are some of the potential problems you face as a church staff leader?

Some of the problems are: time distribution to the various job roles you are asked to assume; maintaining job balance between major and minor projects; robot existence; priority frustration; crises dilemma; dulled creative incentive; self-satisfaction syndrome; role identification; succumbing to the "status quo"; pastor support vacuum; communication breakdown; insufficient office help; insufficient budget; inadequate salary; family situation; job obsolescence; expectations from others; supervisory reporting.

The assignment of supervision carries with it the responsibility for overcoming problems—not just identifying them and explaining *why* they cannot be solved.

Do you understand and accept the concept of staff supervision?

There is confusion and misunderstanding within the ranks of some church staff leaders as to why they report to a staff supervisor. This perplexing dilemma is prompted in the normal course of procedure by the church in "calling" the new worker. His ultimate responsibility is to the church, to be sure, but in order to facilitate team action in attaining the church's goals, the church staff leader's position is "set in" a formal organization of which the pastor is the chief administrator.

When a new staff member, for example, becomes a part of a church staff, his reporting relationship is to the supervisor identified according to the approved organization chart established by the personnel committee.

In order for a church staff to be effective the workers must give more than token acceptance of the principle and function of organization. They must demonstrate quality acceptance.

An employee's negative posture toward organization reporting relationships can seriously impair his attitudes, his work and the effective use of leadership skills in his day-to-day work relationships.

What kind of supervisor-leader are you?

Practically every day brings something new to which human beings must adjust. They turn to you for guidance and help. Under today's pressures, old concepts of leadership are challenged. A leader is no longer a man of great physical strength who imposes his will by sheer force. Rather, workers turn to the person who leads by working with and through them.

To be selected as a supervisor indicates that someone gave credence to your leadership ability or potential.

Writers of articles and books on styles of leaders have coined words and phrases such as leader-centered, group-centered, employee-centered, country club, task oriented, directive, nondirective, human relations oriented, autocratic, paternalistic, laissez-faire, democratic, permissive, participative. Then there is the "I" style, "we" style, and "you" style of leadership.

The above can be grouped generally into five styles of leadership.

• The leader-centered approach. The leader makes the decisions, takes few people into his confidence, and generally keeps authority and responsibility vested in himself. He gives orders and expects them to be obeyed without question. He demands obedience. Workers either shape up or ship out. He is the boss!

• The paternalistic approach. This leader is similar to the one described above, except he assumes a "father knows best" attitude. He sugarcoats all his directives. He does favors for individuals as well as for the group and expects them to be grateful to him. He expects them to carry out his wishes and is offended if they do not—"after all I've done for them."

• The laissez-faire approach. This leader is one who does not take his job seriously. He is the country club type of leader. He is soft in the management of himself and others. His expectations are sacrificed to making employees happy. He lets the group coast along as it will without too much interference or direction. Whatever a worker or the group of workers want to do is OK with him if that is what they want.

• The group-centered approach. This style of leadership involves enhancing the group rather than its leader. The leader uses the available resources of the group to reach the best decisions possible. He demands cooperation. He uses democratic processes.

• The individual-centered approach. This is the "you" style of leadership. The leader deals with workers as individuals as well as in groups. He is interested in quality and quantity production as well as in the peculiar needs of each individual. He invites suggestions and ideas. He uses the participative process in planning projects, goals, and so forth. He stimulates individuals to come up with the best possible solutions to problems or better ways to perform their work. He respects each person as an individual in his own right. When tensions surface, they are acknowledged and dealt with. Attempts are made to challenge each worker to attain his highest potential.

If you do not know which kind of leader you are, your workers do.

The importance of knowing the various types of leadership is to be able to understand and adjust to a new work environment in which you are placed. Especially is this true when moving to a new church field.

For example, suppose the workers in the new field are accustomed to strong directive leadership. Suppose further that your style of leadership is participative. The question arises: How can you graduate your approach and help the workers to change from a directive to a participative leadership? Chances are that if you started by using the democratic process, the workers in the group would not know how to "read" you, would become frustrated, and would want their "old" leader back.

Conversely, a group accustomed to working with a strongly participative leadership will frequently show signs of rebellion when a new leader attempts autocratic domination.

However, even where democracy prevails in a situation, the leader, on occasion, may need to use the authoritarian approach. Leadership styles will vary, depending on the circumstances.

Two main factors in recognizing potentially effective leaders are adventuresomeness and self-concept control. The adventuresome person likes to meet people, is active, genial, friendly, and responsive. He does not feel threatened by others, nor does he feel inferior to them. The second factor, self-concept control, means that he has good feelings about himself. He has self-respect and willpower. He is highly organized in his way of life.

The ultimate test of leadership is the effective accomplishment of a job. However, to judge a person by group effectiveness alone may be unfair. He may be limited by the abilities of the workers under his supervision. Also, a group of highly skilled employees may perform acceptably well even though they are ineffectively led.

Every person has some personal leadership—influence with a fellow worker, a neighbor, a golfing or bowling partner, or members of his own family. Personal influence is desirable, of course, but it does not provide the "thrust" that sustained periods of leadership demand.

Personal leadership may be compared to a parked jet airliner. The passenger capacity and speed statistics are impressive. However, as long as the airplane is parked on the apron, the full potential and purpose of the plane remain dormant. Not until the thrust of the engines moves the plane forward toward planned objectives do the statistics come alive.

Some people live a lifetime on the apron of leadership. They have leadership potential but somehow never learn that they could move out on the runway.

A leader should know the areas in which he is weak, average, or strong. He should know the stimuli which usually cause him satisfaction or irritation. He should know his mannerisms, biases, prejudices, and attitudes which are likely to please or irritate others. He should know his own needs, desires, and life's goals. He should know how changes in his physical states and emotional levels affect his attitudes and should allow for them in dealing rationally with others.

A good leader avoids unnecessary collisions with the views of others. He is a good listener and makes every effort to understand and appreciate the opinions of everyone involved in a situation.

There is nothing magical about leadership. To be a leader requires a constant program of self-discipline, self-analysis, and self-improvement. To lead requires energy and courage and, above all, faith in people. It is almost axiomatic that leaders beget leaders. How fortunate indeed when a group of people have a good leader.

What are leadership skills?

Four of the leadership skills presented in the pages which follow are communicating, listening, delegating, and human relations.

Every person on the church staff needs to consider how much more effective and productive he would be in his work relationships simply by improving his leadership skills.

Some professional workers depend almost entirely upon their academic achievements to carry them through each day's work walk.

Overdependence upon the shingle tends to shackle a person's full use of his capabilities. The sheepskin, an excellent and worthy achievement, will not replace the listening ear, the smile, the greeting, the encouraging word, the hospital visit, and the daily opportunities to express concern, love, and understanding.

When graduation congratulations are over, it's time to get down to work, to discover who you are, your strengths and weaknesses, and what leadership skills you need to develop to become effective and successful in your job speciality.

Communicating is a leadership skill.

As a supervisor or a professional worker, your main job is to get things done through employees as well as volunteer workers. Your plans, ideas, promotions become effective only as you transmit them to others in such a way that they receive (understand) the message intended.

Communication is a process of minds meeting and exchanging understood symbols. Effective listening is an important part of the communication process. You cannot *not* communicate.

As a communicator, you have a known style of communicating facts, ideas, opinions, viewpoints, in face-to-face or problem-solving conferences. The four types are as follows:

• The communicator who is developmental. You encourage two-way conversation. In the planning process, you strive for joint understanding. You don't assume you are right. You encourage exploration and experimentation.

• The communicator who is controlling. You rely on one-way communication. You assume your own ideas and suggestions are best. You try to impose your own viewpoints. You are not interested in alternatives or experimentations.

• The communicator who relinquishes. You assume the other person(s) have more to contribute than you do. You offer few of your own ideas. You are willing to let others experiment on alternatives. You fit in with the other person's viewpoint.

• The communicator who withdraws. You assume "nothing can be done." You avoid interaction, especially conflict. You neither contribute nor ask for suggestions. You are not interested in new approaches or experimentation. You get upset and uptight easily. You may show your displeasure by doodling or walking out.

As a leader, you probably communicate on a face-to-face basis more than in letters, notes, and so on. Oral communication is generally considered to be more effective. This type of communication encourages a two-way process of information exchange and offers fertile ground for new ideas and a means for promoting teamwork.

You are the key person in the communications process. You can talk yourself into trouble; or, by talking things over, you can find a way out of trouble. It is important for most people to talk and to be heard, to voice their requests, ideas, or problems; or to get things off their minds. A really satisfying talk is one of the greatest pleasures there is.

Verbal expression has four main purposes: to give information, to get information, to persuade, and to show human interest in other human beings.

Be sure your actions support your communication. The most persuasive kind of communication is not what you say but what you do. People will tend to discount what you say when your actions or attitudes contradict your words.

Generally, communication which supports the status quo is always easier and more acceptable—and therefore more tempting—than communication which proposes to change the present way of doing things. The leader who innovates may become unpopular, depending largely on how effectively he uses the communications process to lead people from where they are to an acceptance of areas of the unknown or the untried. Communication, then, is a leadership skill, a leadership necessity.

How well do you communicate? Here is a communications checklist which will give you a simple, effective way to size yourself up.

1. Do you assume that your workers know as much about the subject as you do? Aim sharply at their level of knowledge related to the subject or information you are to present. If your workers do not understand you, you are wasting your time and their time.

2. Do you speak words and phrases that have meaning to you but are complete Greek to some of your listeners? Speak words that you know the people will understand. This is not always easy.

3. Do you speak in a dull, sleep-inducing monotone? Vary the pitch and tone of your voice. Vary the pacing—your speed of speaking. You will do this naturally if you are really involved in your work and if you really want to get your story across, whether your purpose be to inform, educate, or resolve a problem.

4. Do you place clear word pictures in the minds of the people as you speak? Be sure you understand the purpose and the planned outcomes of the meeting. Get a clear mental picture of the situation

and frame your thoughts in words that make understandable pictures in the minds of your workers.

5. Do you make transitions smoothly from one subject to another or from one aspect of a subject to another? Let your workers know when you are moving on to another subject or idea.

6. Do you begin speaking immediately about something completely unfamiliar to the workers? Ease into your subject by first stating the familiar and obvious. Get your people oriented and "with you." Make sure they understand you. Then move into the areas that are not so familiar to them. Don't proceed too swiftly. Your voice may sound beautiful to you, and you may have a wonderful feeling of self-satisfaction because you have covered so many points; but you are not succeeding unless the people understand every aspect of your message.

7. Do you get lip and tongue lazy? Realize that words must be heard to be understood. Give each vowel and each consonant its full quality. This doesn't mean "forced" pronunciation. It does mean relaxed formation of words with the equipment God gave you.

8. Do you present your case logically? Mentally arrange the steps from problem to solution or from the familiar to the unfamiliar so that one step naturally leads into the next.

9. Do you shun test runs of your talk or presentation? Review your outline or notes in some quiet place before the meeting begins. Chances are you will make some changes and smooth out the rough spots. Too, this exercise helps to build up your confidence.

10. Do you keep in mind the cardinal rule of communication—the meeting of minds through the exchange of understood symbols? The success of your work as a leader depends on your degree of involvement and understanding of each particular situation and your desire to communicate your message to the workers in a logical, interesting, acceptable, and persuasive manner.

Listening is a leadership skill.

"Why should I tell the minister of education about my leadership problem?" a secretary complained. "He never listens to me anyway."

Do you really listen to what your workers say to you? Your immediate response may be, "Of course I do." But first, reflect upon your own listening habits. Do your physical reactions belie your interest—such actions as not looking directly at the speaker, shifting your weight frequently, doodling, tapping a pencil or pen on the desk, slouching in the chair, jangling the coins in your pocket, cleaning your fingernails, reading, or making personal notes?

Listening is not the same as hearing. Hearing is a physical experience. Listening is a complicated process of absorbing, judging, and acting upon what one hears.

Why is listening so important? For one thing, in the total time spent in the communications process, persons spend more time in listening than in reading, writing, or speaking.

For another thing, people naturally gravitate toward those who respect them as human beings, who make them feel secure, who try to understand their point of view. The main job of the leader is to get the job done through others. One of the best ways to achieve all this is through listening.

Why have some leaders developed poor listening habits? Among the reasons is that few people have been trained to listen. People learn to listen the way they learn to walk. At an early age they start to do what comes naturally.

Another reason is that the brain can work faster than the mouth. Thinking is much faster than speaking. Consequently, the listener's brain usually engages in "rabbit chasing" that impedes concentration and comprehension. What the other person says simply does not get through.

Cultivating the art of listening may not, by itself, make a leader; but you will find very few leaders who are not experts at listening.

Listening promotes understanding.

Listening helps resolve complaints.

Listening encourages and collects ideas.

Listening aids persuasion.

How well do you listen? Here is a listening self-checklist which will give you a simple, effective way to size yourself up.

1. Do you decide even before the person speaks, based on previous conversations, that what he has to say is unimportant? Your experiences of past conversations with a worker are not always a true indicator of his present needs. Always relate to every person in a friendly, helpful manner.

2. Do you mentally criticize his clothes, his haircut, or anything

else about him? Mentally criticizing is cruelly unfair. Give complete attention to the *person* and hear what he has to say.

3. Do you listen only for facts? Although facts are important, you should also listen for words expressing positive or negative emotional tones. You should also use your extra thinking time to question whether the speaker is skirting an obvious fact or leaving an argument dangling.

4. Do you fake attention? You can't really get by with faking attention. In time your people will tab you as a "nonlistener." Too, your credibility as a leader may be damaged.

5. Do you mentally line up arguments to counter what is said? Spending your mental time lining up counter arguments or framing your next remarks precludes full attention to the speaker. This does not mean to make no mental notes for recall for clarification and discussion.

6. Do you know your own prejudices? If you make an effort to discount them, you will be able to distinguish between the speaker and his conversation.

7. Do you allow "trigger words" to set off irrational reactions? The better you know the words that have "loaded" meanings for you, the less emotional impact there will be between you and the people you lead.

8. Do you ask questions for clarification? However, hold your questions until the speaker finishes saying what is on his mind.

9. Do you keep an open mind? Don't prejudice the outcome, regardless of the subject material. When you make up your mind in advance, you will miss pertinent facts and frustrate understanding.

10. Do you make sure you understand the speaker? If you are not sure you understood the speaker, briefly restate what you *think* you heard and ask, "Is that what you mean?"

11. Do you practice the discipline of concentration? Learn to concentrate. Fatigue, lack of incentive, and insufficient practice are most often responsible for inattentive listening.

12. Do you create distractions during the conversation? A problem, a complaint, or a request for help is a very important matter to the speaker. Do not employ diversionary tactics, innocently or not, to draw attention away from the problem. For example, do not say, "That reminds me of an incident when I was a child." Listen to *him*. You may not be able to help, but you can show by listening that you understand. That helps.

Delegating is a leadership skill.

A number of supervisors as well as nonsupervisors find themselves in a quandary of so much to do and so little time. But not so, if you know what and how to delegate.

As a staff worker, your main job is to do the planning—unilaterally or with others—but to get the job done through others. That involves delegating.

Delegation means the giving or assigning to others the responsibility and authority to make certain decisions and to perform certain tasks on your behalf.

Delegation requires great skill and judgment. Although it involves you, as supervisor, to assign part of your authority to another person to make decisions, it does not relieve you of the final responsibility for the decisions he makes.

You acquired your own authority through the delegating process. You, in turn, must know how to use it in redelegating part of your job to the workers you supervise.

Several reasons why some staff workers are reluctant to delegate are:

• "I believe in the saying 'If you want a thing done well, do it yourself.' " This attitude is deeply rooted for many persons. It must change if the church staff leader is to multiply himself through others.

• "I was disappointed in the results." It's possible adequate controls were not established.

• "I had to finish the job." It's possible the job was not challenging or was beyond the capabilities of the delegate. Or, the staff person failed to give clear instructions.

• "It would take more time for me to instruct the worker than to do it myself." This may be true. However, if it is a recurring task, wisdom dictates the value of a one-time instruction session.

Another reason for going sour on delegating is that professional workers tried it at the wrong time. They became job-pressured so they delegated. The time to delegate is before you have to.

Advantages of delegating are:

> Relieves you of the less important routine duties
> Gives you more time to spend on goals and projects that demand your immediate attention

Releases you to give more attention to the professional aspects of your job

Helps build a more effective work team

Helps to develop workers to solve problems and make decisions

Helps to build trust and cooperation

What should you delegate to your workers?

- Delegate details that recur. Ask yourself these questions:
  What keeps repeating itself in my job?
  What minor decisions do I make most frequently?
  What job details take the biggest single "chunk" of my time?

- Delegate for personal development. Ask these questions:
  What parts of my job am I least qualified to perform?
  What job details do I dislike most?
  What job tasks that I perform make me under-specialized?

What should you not delegate to your workers?

• You do not delegate general supervisory duties and actions involved in planning, organizing, directing, and evaluating the work. You do not delegate major decision-making. You do not delegate to others the responsibility to develop the workers you supervise.

- You do not delegate policy formulation.
- You do not delegate disciplinary matters.
- You do not delegate employee promotions, transfers, etc.
- You do not delegate salary plan decisions.
- You do not delegate employee work performance reviews.

How do you delegate?

This is a knotty question for many supervisors. These suggestions may be helpful.

- Delegate to people you can trust.
- Match delegation to a worker's special abilities.
- Delegate a whole task—not just a piece of it.
- Delegate clearly and concisely—in writing, if necessary.
- Delegate to develop employees.
- Delegate to the lowest level at which a job can be done.
- State the results you require, but let the employee work out his own way of achieving them.

- Warn the worker of pitfalls, if the nature of the assignment requires it.
- Explain the limits of his authority, if applicable.
- Don't delegate authority to one person you have already delegated to someone else.
- Don't delegate, and then, by discussing limitations and restrictions of his use of authority, make the worker reluctant to tackle the job.
- Don't delegate to the impairment of overall staff morale.

How can you maintain control once you have delegated?

This question poses the dilemma that frightens some supervisors from using the leadership skill of delegating. Here are some ways to maintain control.

- Maintain friendly, open communication.
- Follow up. From time to time, ask workers how their projects are going.
- Establish deadlines.
- Make occasional spot checks of progress.
- Keep the workers informed on any changes that might affect tasks delegated to them.

A decision to delegate *is* risky. However, most of the risks the supervisor takes will be to his advantage.

Human relations is a leadership skill.

You may know the academic and professional aspects of your job from "here to yonder" and from "top to bottom," but if you don't have the ability of getting along with people, your efforts and your results are about as effective as a "paper tiger." The most successful leaders on your staff and in your church are those who have good people relationships.

Human relations is people. Working effectively and productively with people is a skill that can be learned. Human relations is knowing how to handle difficult people problems; understanding the motivations of other people as well as your own; and building sound working relationships with many kinds of people.

Human relations is not manipulation. No one likes to be the victim of some underhanded maneuver. When it is used, the person or persons manipulated usually lose interest in the project or goal and respect for the supervisor or leader.

A human relations climate is not built upon a mass approach.

It is built upon a person-to-person relationship. It is an individual matter. Each worker senses your personal warmth and concern, your depth of commitment of fair play by the way you consistently respond to him as a person.

You do not build good human relations in a day or week or month. It's the long haul of days upon days of relationship consistency that ultimately forms your human relations climate. You don't determine when that time arrives; your workers do.

In fact, building good human relationships may not be so much learning how to get along with others as taking the kinks out of yourself so that others can get along with you.

A good principle to follow in developing good human relations is to decide beforehand how you are going to relate to a certain person rather than how you think he should relate to you.

The feelings of people are fragile.

How do you develop good human relations to bring out the best in people?

How does a person feel when, after one or more years on the job, you still call him by the wrong name?

What would be an employee's work attitude if, time after time, good work on assignments had been done and you never had said, "That was a good job"?

Or, how long could a person tolerate a situation where every voiced desire was an order, or a demand, instead of a request?

Or, how would one feel after returning from an extended illness you hardly recognized his presence?

Little things! And, perhaps they are. But somehow it's the little things done by a supervisor on a day-to-day basis that people remember and which contribute greatly to bringing out their best. For some supervisors, this is an enigma.

There is a big difference in being thoughtful of others—showing common courtesies—and pampering them.

Supervisors often show by small acts of commission or omission that they are not really interested in each person as an individual. Workers become keenly aware and resentful of their seeming robot existence. Some supervisors are tight-lipped with their words of praise. When deserved praise is not expressed, the worker's motivations to perform efficiently are appreciably dulled.

Yet other supervisors create an atmosphere of fear as a motivation for getting the work done. Whether or not the supervisor does so intentionally makes little difference to the worker who daily feels fear pressures. Generally, people do not perform at their best under an umbrella of fear.

The attitude of the supervisor is extremely important—attitude in terms of people as they are related to their work. A good supervisor knows he can develop a better team when he blends an employee-centered and production-centered style of leadership. However, the supervisor who attempts to substitute a superficial interest in the worker in order to get production is not fooling anyone but himself. The workers detect insincerity and resent being used in this way.

How can supervisors, who come in all shapes and sizes, who bring to their jobs certain specific knowledge and skills, and who have varying attitudes, emotions, likes, and dislikes, bring out the best in people? Here are several suggestions:

- Show a genuine interest in workers. To know their names is not enough; know their problems also. Understand workers and their reactions. Provide opportunity for employee development and self-improvement. Show patience, tolerance, and understanding. Treat workers as human beings. Show respect for their feelings. A friendly manner and kindly guidance win cooperation. When you show a genuine interest in people, they usually respond through improved work attitude and production.

- Communicate clearly. Nothing is quite so frustrating to a worker as garbled instruction. Result: waste of time and loss of job motivation. On the other hand, clear, easily understood instructions create mutual confidence between the worker and the supervisor. Job confidence is a requisite to top performance.

- Observe rules of courtesy. A "please" makes the assignment seem less like an order or a demand. The words "thank you" require no extra effort, but pave the way for heartier cooperation. Courtesy promotes mutual respect, goodwill, and helps greatly to bring out the best in people.

- Criticize in the right way. No one likes to be criticized openly where others can hear. A good supervisor does not cause a worker to lose face or self-respect. He criticizes in private. He criticizes in a constructive manner. He always leaves the person thinking well of himself. If the supervisor has no ready answer or solution, he should probably remain silent until he does.

- Give credit where credit is due. When you give credit to

another, you gain credit yourself. A supervisor who does not praise those with whom he works soon finds himself working twice as hard and getting less cooperation. A worker sometimes expresses appreciation for a fellow employee. Such consideration is commendable. However, nothing satisfies quite as much as when the supervisor says, "Thank you for the good job you did."

• Let each worker know where he stands. Periodically discuss performance evaluations.

• Inform workers in advance of changes which affect them. They want to be "in" on things. They show their appreciation by being more effective.

• Know all your workers personally. Find out their interests, habits, and touchy points. Capitalize on your knowledge of them.

• Fulfill promises. A good supervisor is careful about the promises he makes. However, once he makes a promise, he must keep it in order to be known as a man of his word.

• Resolve complaints promptly and fairly. A problem or complaint of a worker should be very real and important to you. The worker wants an explanation, an answer, or action. He is quite sensitive to the degree of your interest and willingness to set up an appointment to discuss the matter. Arrange a time for private talk as soon as possible. Listen to the worker. Resolve the complaint or problem in a way that is fair to *all* concerned. The worker with the complaint may or may not agree with the solution. However, the more important questions are: Does this worker feel that he received a fair hearing? Does he feel that another worker with the same complaint would have received the same answer?

• Treat workers impartially. Perhaps no one act of the supervisor breaks down morale more quickly than showing favoritism. To give one worker a day off now and then but to refuse others the same privilege invites problems by the dozen. Acts of favoritism, however subtle, create conflict, antagonism, and cause a general breakdown of morale. The good supervisor brings out the best in people by impartial and considerate treatment.

• Treat workers fairly. Supervisors are sometimes confused in their dealings with other humans. In the turmoil created by unexpected situations, their confusion is somewhat like that of the man who stepped off the curb while the traffic light was changing. In that brief moment, a motorist, who speeded up to get across the intersection, splashed him with mud and water. As the man jumped back on the curb, he exclaimed excitedly to two bystanders, "Did you two fools see what that gentleman just did to me?"

He was confused, but no more mixed up than are some supervisors in everyday situations which made sudden demands to deal fairly with people.

A person's estimate or measure of his own sense of fairness may or may not be in agreement with those whom he supervises. Workers are sensitive to observable or knowledgeable inequities in so-called fair treatment.

Most supervisors would rate high on some of the *major* aspects of fair treatment of others. Some examples are: not telling a deliberate falsehood about a fellow worker; not intentionally assigning the hardest job to a certain employee to hasten his termination; or not knowingly claiming credit for something a worker under his supervision accomplished.

But how would these same supervisors rate when *little* things that count for so much are involved? Such as:

Criticizing a worker for a mistake when inquiry reveals that he had not been adequately instructed;

Making a careless remark about a worker before another and thus creating adverse opinion;

Deciding not to give an employee a salary increase because of one recent unfavorable incident;

Calling together all the workers to reprimand them collectively when only one is at fault; or,

Giving one employee his choice of vacation time and then asking the others to choose their times so as not to be in conflict.

The achievement of fairness in both big and little things requires constant striving. Intent is involved, of course, but intent in itself is not enough. There is no halfway in fairness.

Another important area affecting human relations involves the fair treatment of all employees in the administration of the church's employee benefit plan.

Although an employee may be unhappy to find that the benefits he receives are less than those received by workers in other churches, his real discontent is caused by the knowledge that he is not treated the same as other workers in his own group. Confidence of fair treatment is of prime concern to the employee.

When is a worker treated unfairly in the administration of employee benefits? Generally speaking, unfairness results when no rhyme or reason exists to explain why one or more workers are excluded from some staff benefits, or why there are wide variances in benefits to be shared by all. A worker who does not understand the employee benefit plan may not raise his voice to question a seeming inequity. However, quiet acceptance does not necessarily imply happy acceptance. No one likes to be treated unfairly. One of the major "wants" of every employee is to work in a place where he is treated fairly. Such treatment helps to bring out the best in people.

• Admit your mistakes. The sign on the desk read: You may go home now—you've already made enough mistakes for one day.

What an easy way to solve problems! If going home would erase the mistakes, going home is sound advice. However, the mistakes of the day, week, or month have a way of shadowing us wherever we go.

A mistake is the result of misjudgment. Misjudgments are risks taken in decision-making, and church supervisors make decisions every day. Some are major decisions; others are minor. Some supervisors base their decisions on hunches or personal prejudices which cloud rational, logical thinking.

Other supervisors make decisions off the cuff. They do not know exactly why they make them, and not until later, when the decision backfires or when a study of facts reveals a better decision, is the earlier judgment labeled a mistake. Sometimes a person must make a serious blunder before he will take self-inventory. For the moment at least, he knows he does not want to make that same mistake again.

No one deliberately wants to make mistakes, but everyone makes them. Some people make more than others. In fact, there are those who seem to be mistake-prone as some are accident-prone. The harder they try not to make mistakes, the more they seem to make.

However, most people are sympathetic with the misjudgments that staff supervisors make, and try to be understanding. This is fortunate. There comes a time, though, when sympathy and understanding are somewhat strained.

How do employees of a church staff react to a supervisor who is guilty of recurring mistakes? Here are some possible evaluations:

He is incapable of learning from his mistakes.

He uses poor judgment.

He is indecisive.

Fortunately, most supervisors have discovered that they can learn from their own mistakes as well as from the mistakes of others. Here are some suggestions to aid in this learning process:

Admit the mistake. Acknowledging a mistake is the first step toward correction, improvement, and development. Mistakes can be good teachers. Workers respect the supervisor who is courageous enough to admit it when he is wrong.

Analyze the mistake. Think a while about a recent blunder that was made. Did pressure force a decision? Some decisions require time for thinking, weighing facts, and anticipating possible consequences. Was pressure the reason for misjudgment? Do not be pressured into hasty decisions merely out of a desire to appear decisive to a fellow worker or church member. Ask for additional information if necessary, or say specifically that more time is needed to think things through. A supervisor must make many minor decisions daily as problems arise.

Remember that one's mental or physical condition on the day of the decision could be a possible clue.

Reflect upon the circumstances that immediately preceded the instance of judgment. Were they important? Would the same mistake probably be made under similar circumstances? The successful supervisor tries to undo mistakes, but not before carefully analyzing them.

Consider the nature of the error. How serious is the mistake? Will it affect others? If so, to what extent? Should you disregard the error? And if you do, will the mistake take root and grow?

Sometimes the overly conscientious person broods over and bemoans all his mistakes. Such an attitude affects his overall work. He subconsciously becomes indecisive for fear of making other mistakes. He creates a false leadership.

Conversely, the effective supervisor is concerned. He studies carefully the nature of each error and boldly faces the consequences. Once a decision is reached, he acts.

If necessary, discuss the mistake with your own supervisor. This involves judgment. When admission of error to supervisor or pastor becomes necessary, try to think in terms of him and the church, rather than yourself. He wants to know the nature of the mistake, its results, and what is proposed as an alternate. Out of this experience of sharing feelings usually comes understanding and support.

To learn from mistakes may mean a revision of past decisions when similar problems or situations arose. Revising decisions when one is shown to be wrong takes courage. Usually, people tend to forget past errors when one shows by current decisions that he has learned by his mistakes.

How well do you get along with others?

Here is a human relations checklist which will give you an effective way to size yourself up.

1. Are you generally cheerful? Grouchiness and irritability dampen the spirit and enthusiasm of everyone with whom you come in contact. A pleasant, cheerful disposition works wonders as a mortar to bind people together.

2. Do you manage to keep calm under pressure? A person who cannot control himself can hardly hope to control others. Self-control under all circumstances gives that poise and sureness which commands respect.

3. Do you keep the promises you make? Promises should not be made lightly. When you promise anything, do everything you can to deliver.

4. Do you tend to be impatient? Patience is an essential quality in working with people. Being impatient with people tends to create confusion and frustration and often plants seeds of resentment.

5. Do you violate personal confidences? Violating a confidence has the same effect as a broken promise, except that the resentment is often more intense. You reduce your effectiveness as a leader when people feel that you can't keep a confidence. They may question your integrity in other areas of work relationships.

6. Do you give credit where credit is due? Don't hog all the credit when something nice happens. Give commendation to a person when he does a good job.

7. Do you make an effort to be a good listener? When you listen, you get a better understanding of what is on the other person's mind. Don't permit your verbal, facial, or physical reactions to express your "pre-conclusions." Doing so shows lack of respect for his feelings and opinions.

8. Do you ignore complaints which appear insignificant to you? No complaint is insignificant to the person who is making it. The complaint may be unjustified in your opinion, but your inattention will only aggravate the situation.

9. Can you refuse a person's request without ill will? An abrupt

no to a request is sure to arouse irritation. One way to handle such a delicate situation is to begin by saying: "I know exactly how you feel, and there have been times when I have felt the same way; but . . ." Then tactfully and courteously tell the person why you cannot honor his request.

10. Do you ever ask for opinions and suggestions? Asking for suggestions brings more people into the act. When you ask a person what he thinks, you plant in him the seeds of self-assurance and self-satisfaction and also enhance his feeling of "belonging."

11. Do you make sarcastic remarks? It is easy to commit this grave error when you are defensive. Sarcasm makes workers feel inferior and produces resentment. A leader who uses sarcasm as a way to influence persons is deficient in leadership ability.

12. Do you speak in a loud and commanding voice? People generally tend to shy away from the person who has this style of leadership—not because they are afraid of him, but because he makes them nervous and sometimes angry. Develop an informal, warm manner of speaking that is pleasant to listen to and also to respond to.

13. Do you have a positive attitude? It is difficult for other people to work with anyone who has a negative attitude, and they are less apt to be interested in cooperating with you. When you are positive, you are energetic, highly motivated, productive, and alert. A positive attitude seems to open the gate for inner enthusiasm.

14. Do you make snap judgments in sizing up people? The best cure for this disease is to recall some of the horrible injustices placed on other people because of some whim, bias, or caprice of the moment. The best approach, which builds good human relations, is to look for the good things in each person and to accentuate the positive. This approach makes for zestful living. It is Christlike.

15. Are you a moody person? A leader who is changeable, impulsive, melancholy, downcast, irritable, or crabbed is hard to work with. People like to work with a leader whose general, positive behavior and disposition can be predicted.

16. Do you admit your own mistakes? A mistake is a misjudgment. We all make misjudgments. Admit your own mistakes. People will respect you for doing so.

17. Do you always say please and thank you? Practice the discipline of courtesy. The leader who is polite, gentle, affable, gracious, and mannerly in his behavior exemplifies the spirit of Christ.

Christian ethics and discourtesy are incompatible.

18. Are you skillful in giving explanations and information? Your success depends a great deal upon your ability to speak so that people know what you mean. Clarify in your own mind what you want to say to a person or to a group of people. Ask for feedback to get mutual understanding.

19. Do you argue? Don't argue. You may win your point but lose your co-worker's goodwill. Always respect every person's right to his own opinions.

20. Do you keep postponing requests from your workers? The greatest thief of time is procrastination. Not only is it a sign of weakness on the part of a leader, it creates and compounds frustration for workers. If a person makes a request which requires some checking, tell him so. Then follow through.

Human relations is more than smiling at people. Working with people requires leadership skill. Basic attitudes which comprise a philosophy of life are more significant than the techniques used. However, techniques used appropriately and sincerely are highly endorsed and encouraged.

Human relations is more than giving service to church members. Service without heart, understanding, and personal interest is like tinkling silver and sounding brass.

Human relations is not achieved by status: a walnut desk, carpet, and matched appointments. Human relations is not achieved with things; but rather, they exist between people. An attractive and orderly office is helpful in creating a climate for giving efficient and friendly service, of course. But when a person depends upon things to give him status, he tends to grow inward and become dwarfed.

Few people attain high levels in human relations skills. Yet the rules are so simple that they can be used easily by anyone who sincerely desires to improve. However, it is one thing to know the rules and quite another to apply them. The supervisor's success in human relations skills waits upon putting desire into action.

"Finally, you must all live in harmony, be sympathetic, loving as brothers, tenderhearted, humble, never returning evil for evil or abuse for abuse, but blessing instead" (1 Pet. 3: 8–9, Williams).

9
How to Plan and Conduct Staff Meetings

When someone asked a small boy the purpose of a cow's hide, he replied, "To hold the cow together." In a very real sense, one outcome of good staff meetings is to hold the staff together. These meetings can form an integral part of the work life of paid employees by binding them together as a unit. Staff meetings can give purpose and direction to the overall work of the staff.

Although fellowship is involved, the purpose of staff meetings is for more than fellowship; or for devotional services, as important as they are; or for checking the weekly calendar of activities; or for reviewing the results of the past Sunday.

Basically, a staff meeting is a medium of communication. It is not an end in itself; it is a means to an end. However, a meeting of the staff should not be used for every communication situation which arises among workers. There are times when a memo serves the purpose or talking individually to those specifically concerned with a work problem may be better.

The optimum value of a staff meeting lies in the change it produces in the participants such as knowledge, attitude, behavior, work habits, and to spark self-development goals.

Someone has said, "We keep minutes, but waste hours." Another has commented, "A camel is a horse put together by a committee." These two observations reveal a simple fact: some meetings are a waste of time, poorly planned and nonproductive. An example is calling a meeting to decide something you could or should decide yourself.

Someone hopefully mused, "If some conference leaders were laid end to end, it would probably be a good thing."

Conferences can be frustrating and emotionally draining experiences.

"Daddy must not feel so well,"
  The child was heard to say.
"Your daddy's been to a meeting, dear;
  He's had it for today."

Or, conferences can be stimulating, motivating, and productive. "Living together a lot in a short time" expresses the healthy interaction that should pervade a problem-solving session.

What are some negative attitudes toward staff meetings?

- Expressed by the conference leaders:

Planning takes too much time.
Regular meeting schedules are burdensome.
We don't have enough things to talk about.
We really don't need meetings. Staff members and I talk informally from time to time.
Every worker has his own job description. He knows what to do.
I can't seem to get around to having them.
I've tried, but we've got two fellows who always hassle, and I've decided not to have another staff meeting until they make up or leave.

- Expressed by the conferees:

The leader often calls meetings on short notice.
It is evident the leader makes little or no plans for the meeting.
The leader has already arrived at the solution of the problem.
The leader monopolizes the discussion.
Little things absorb the time. We never get to the big items.
We ramble too much.
We talk a lot but do little.
We chase too many rabbits.
We seldom start on time.
The leader attempts to answer all the questions.
We just seem to go on and on . . .

Why have staff meetings?

Are they worth the time and effort? The answer is a positive *yes*. Purposeful staff meetings are extremely important to the support of the overall church program cycle of planning, organizing, leading, and evaluating projects and activities.

In fact, churches which have few or no staff meetings may be having staff problems of all sorts. There must be a formal plan of internal staff communication to coordinate the total work of the staff, to increase productivity, and for the church to realize the benefits of the expertise of staff leadership. There are several reasons for conducting staff meetings:

    To solve a problem
    To give, share, and clarify information
    To coordinate efforts
    To make and review plans and schedules
    To evaluate results
    To utilize group thinking
    To create—come up with innovations and new ideas
    To decide on best use of available resources (people, materials, and facilities, budget, time)

What are some outcomes of good staff meetings?

• They help to positionize and identify each staff member as a part of the team. He feels that he belongs. His identity as a team member is important to him. Staff meetings help him get into the act.

• They serve as a mortar to hold the group together. Good rapport is basic to concerted action.

• They encourage employee self-development. Out of group interaction often come incentives which motivate workers to pursue further study in their field, or related fields of work.

• They help participants discover new goal possibilities in their own work.

• They help staff supervisors (minister of education, church business administrator, and so forth) to plan and conduct acceptably staff meetings with their own workers.

Who is responsible for staff meetings?

The pastor is responsible for planning and conducting meetings comprising the total paid staff or any segment of it as required to accomplish the meeting's objectives.

Each supervisor, such as the minister of education, church business administrator, minister of music, is responsible for planning and conducting necessary meetings involving the workers he supervises directly.

How often should you schedule staff meetings?

As often as needed is a good answer to this question, but it may not be the best one. There are some pastors, or other staff supervisors who seldom, if ever, plan staff meetings, because they personally feel no need for them. Usually, none of the others on the staff shares this feeling. In fact, in some churches where there are no staff meetings, the workers usually say to one another, "If we could just get together once in a while to solve some of our work problems," or "If we just knew what was going on," or "Maybe we could do a better job if all of us were pulling in the same direction."

Two extremes seem to exist; not having any meetings, or scheduling them daily or weekly without preplanning. To the question, When do you hold staff meetings? a survey disclosed these responses:

> We do not have staff meetings
> No special time
> Whenever a staff meeting is needed
> Every Monday morning
> Once a month

A few churches in the survey indicated a regular daily session. By far the greatest percent indicated that they held regular weekly meetings. Every day in the work week was mentioned, but Monday was the most popular time. According to this survey, comparatively few staff meetings were held in the afternoon. The morning hours between 8:30—11:00 were most frequently named.

What are the elements of a staff meeting?

The four elements of a staff meeting are:

> Planning for the staff meeting
> Conducting the meeting
> Getting involvement and participation
> Evaluating the results

How do you plan staff meetings?

Planning is sometimes considered merely as an activity rather than a mental process.

Planning is sometimes confused with scheduling—selecting a place for the meeting, deciding on the time, and getting out the notices.

The ultimate success of a staff meeting depends largely on how well you plan for the meeting. Your planning effort will achieve results of greater value than the time it took to plan.

Some leaders prepare excellent agendas beforehand, but become slaves to their planning by holding doggedly to the agenda, even though other important items may surface during the meeting.

Sometimes leaders are labeled as autocratic because they do come to the meeting with a planned agenda and stick to the meeting's main purposes.

Having an agenda is not in itself autocratic. Keeping the discussion organized and moving is not autocratic. The leader is not autocratic when he speaks at length on a subject about which he alone is knowledgeable. The leader is not autocratic when he encourages workers who monopolize the discussion to talk less.

The real challenge for staff leaders who conduct meetings is to give thoughtful consideration to the following planning suggestions:

• Define the meeting's purpose. Think through these questions: Why have this meeting? What do we hope to accomplish in this meeting? Keep in mind that, since a meeting serves only as a medium of communication, the actual results are usually reached later, not at the meeting itself.

When the reason for the meeting is determined, write it down. If a problem is to be solved, be sure to state it clearly. The agenda may include more than one purpose of the meeting. Be sure you provide a communication bridge in moving from one purpose to another.

• Get facts beforehand. They may be readily available from the files, or they may require research. Do not assume that without prior notice a worker in the meeting will have all the facts at his fingertips. Not only is the delay in getting facts a waste of the time of those who wait, but it is also a source of embarrassment to the person who was not able to produce information "off the cuff." When a meeting continues without vital facts, the conferees may reach an impasse, or debate in circles, or make a decision on the basis of guesswork.

Not every meeting requires the gathering of factual information beforehand. Planning, however, can spotlight the need for this or for other areas of advance preparation.

• Determine the type of meeting to be conducted. The role which the leader assumes in the meeting depends largely on the objectives to be accomplished. Is the purpose of the meeting to inform ("tell and sell") of a decision already made, or to pool considered opinions, ideas, and facts for decision-making, or for collecting information?

Each type (to inform and persuade, or to solve a problem) requires a different leadership role. For example, if the purpose of the meeting is to inform others of a decision already reached by the leader, or by a church committee, one simply tells the workers what was decided. In this instance, the meeting is informational. The leader's role, basically, is one of relaying instructions, explaining decisions or actions already formulated, answering the conferee's questions, and motivating (sell) the participant to acceptance. In this type of meeting, counterarguments or suggestions for possible improvement by the conferees are out of place. The matter is already settled. It is entirely possible that if counter-proposals are offered by the conferees, the leader, at the beginning, did not communicate clearly to them the purpose of the meeting.

If the purpose of the meeting is to solve a problem, the leader assumes a different role. He states the problem, gives opportunity for discussion, examines the facts, hears possible solutions, and either selects the best solution and an alternate, or shares this responsibility with the group. See next page for seating arrangement and communication flow in various types of meetings.

• Determine who should attend the staff meeting.
The purpose of the meeting determines who should attend. If it is principally for devotion and fellowship, especially at the beginning of the session, perhaps all paid workers, including the custodians and maids, should be present.

However, if the purpose is for matters such as: to solve a problem, make plans, hear progress reports, or coordinate projects and activities, then only those staff members who have definite responsibilities in these areas should attend. They are the ones qualified to

SUGGESTED ARRANGEMENT OF TABLES AND CHAIRS

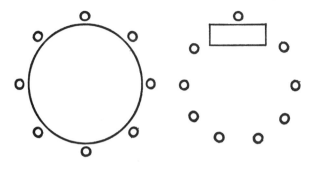

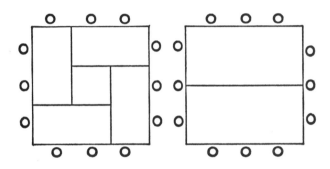

GROUP INTERACTION

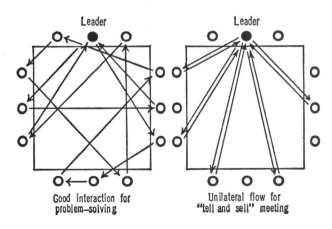

Good interaction for
problem-solving

Unilateral flow for
"tell and sell" meeting

have opinions. They are the workers who have the facts, or who are in charge of a project, or who will carry out group decisions, or whose work becomes involved later on.

A poor stewardship of time is to ask clerical workers to sit through an hour's session involving discussion which is of little or no interest to them. If "sitting through the meeting" is required of all staff members, some of the clerical workers will certainly develop an apathetic attitude toward them. They can't wait to get back to their work, especially if it is piled high on their desks.

On the other hand, if an item on the agenda involves developing better interoffice communication procedure, the clerical workers, especially those who answer the telephones, should be present to participate in the discussion. After the matter is settled, the clerical workers can be excused to return to their desks.

On a smaller church staff comprising three, four, or five workers, the pastor may wish all workers to remain for the entire session, largely because of the close relationship and interrelated work involvements.

It is the responsibility of the pastor (or the supervisor for his own group) to arrange the time and place of the meeting. Choose a place with ample space, good lighting, chairs, and chalkboard. Select a room away from the telephone, if possible.

Notify the workers in advance of the meeting date. Tell them the purpose of the meeting if there are problems to discuss.

• Prepare an agenda. Examine its contents carefully for clarity and completeness, especially if you distribute it prior to the meeting. Most disagreements occur because people are not talking about the same thing.

• Ask someone to take minutes of the meeting.

• Another important item in preparing for the meeting is to get together necessary materials such as records, charts, pamphlets, chalk, eraser, pencils, paper.

How do you conduct a staff meeting?

Some staff meetings start about like this: "We better go ahead without the others. We have a number of things to talk about and perhaps you're as pressed for time as I am."

Or, "If you all don't mind waiting a few moments, I have a couple of long distance telephone calls to make."

The principles of conducting a successful conference are:

Creating a warm environment.
Getting involvement and participation.
Giving guidance.
Keeping the meeting moving in the direction intended.

Although thorough preparation is necessary for an effective meeting, that alone does not ensure success. There must be purposeful participation by all members. The mutual give and take (interactions) of the conferees, their awareness, sensitivity, and diagnostic skill—all these largely determine the success of a meeting.

To increase the chances for a successful meeting, add to good preparation these suggestions:

• Preside gracefully. Courtesy, good manners, and efficiency complement one another.

• Start on time. Begin with prayer.

• Define the type of meeting: informational, problem-solving or other. Or, if it is a multi-purpose meeting, identify each type as your proceed through the agenda.

• Open the discussion. Group discussion is the base upon which action is built by the church staff, church council, and committee.

To get the discussion started, ask pertinent questions to arouse interest and provoke thinking. The leader does not necessarily need to be an expert on the subject for discussion. Rather, he should be skilled in the use of the participative process. Asking the right questions helps keep the discussion moving.

The purpose of questions is not only to open the discussion, but to stimulate interest, accumulate or verify data, distribute participation, change discussion direction, and to arrive at conclusions. For example, if the group seems to be deadlocked in finding alternate solutions ask, What will happen if we decide to go this way?

Questions can be grouped into three kinds: the *overhead* question directed to all participants; the *direct* question directed to one person and the *throwback* question directed to the group to avoid giving your own opinions.

Some leaders employ a pseudodemocratic method in leading a problem-solving conference. This means that the leader already has the solution in mind. He merely goes through the motions of a participative process. By pulling from the conferees an opinion which, in reality, voices his predetermined solution, he hopes to make them think that it is theirs. This manipulation is deeply resented by the participants when it is discovered.

When a problem-solving meeting is so identified, the leader must proceed honestly with the group and follow the participative process toward reaching a decision. If he has ideas to contribute, he should present them for evaluation and discussion, but not in a manner to make others feel that he is structuring the meeting.

Reluctance on the part of the leader to trust the mental capacities of others prompts them to distrust the leader.

• Get everyone into the act. Encourage participation and mutual exchange of experiences, opinions, and ideas. Create an atmosphere in which each one feels free to take part in the discussion.

It is not your place as the leader to talk often or at length, unless, of course, you are presenting new information. Your purpose is to get others to feel unrestrained in presenting their ideas, comments, and suggestions.

How do you secure group interaction? How do you lead the group to look carefully at all four corners of a problem? How do you lead them to a quality group decision?

These questions have no "pat" answers. You must reckon with a wide gamut of individual differences. A person may be a recognized leader in one situation and a lukewarm participant in another. Each conferee relates in varied and peculiar ways both to the leader and to the group. Because of the diversity of individual differences inherent in any group, conflict and controversy are potentially present.

The successful conference leader recognizes that personal freedom is important to creativity. However, leaders may limit the creative freedom of conferees by allowing negative aspects—such as conformity, passivity, mediocrity, or manipulation—of group thinking to dominate the meeting.

For example, the response of the leader or conferee to the suggestion of another participant may be, "But that's not the way we've been doing it," or "We always promote this activity in March." The fact that the project has never quite succeeded in March seemingly has made little impact on some of the participants. For them the die is cast. They are slaves to conformity.

How can you unshackle a group from these slavish conference habits? How can you stimulate and control a healthy exchange of ideas? The following suggestions may be helpful:

1. Develop a participative, cooperative style of leadership. This

leadership style has a liberating effect on others, while the autocratic leader stifles and limits discussion. The participative leader is interested in the creative freedom of conferees, in member interaction, in reaching the best group decisions, and in having participants satisfy their personal needs.

In such an atmosphere, discussion and interaction take place freely. In this environment, leadership is shared. The various abilities inherent in a group suggest the possibility that it can reach quality decisions and arrive at better solutions than an individual is able to do alone. Your own interest in every person and his contributions should be constantly evident.

2. Maintain group interaction until the participants are ready for a group decision. Accept contributions, facts, comments, ideas, or questions from any conferee. Let each individual discuss his solution to the problem. A conference group in which the members identify with one another is usually one in which interpersonal relations are conducive to quality problem-solving.

Encourage those with adverse ideas to speak out. Everyone needs to understand the thinking of each person. When conflicting ideas produce sharp controversy, the leader steps in to restate each person's opinion in a way that is satisfactory to those involved. Usually, this action clarifies arguments and produces understanding.

A group without differences of opinion and conflict may be in serious trouble. When points of view are withheld, the best solution may never be reached.

The leader, as well as the conferees, must understand that a participant's differing opinion is not necessarily personal. When this fact is understood, the problem can be dealt with by the group, free from emotional involvement. Personality conflicts are often difficult to resolve. Generally, the meeting ends in an impasse. The leader, then, must develop habits and skills in his conference behavior (speaking and listening) which encourage conferees to express freely their differing points of view.

Sometimes conflict and controversy result from deficiencies in language and communication skills, particularly in the inability of some conferees to interpret and weigh facts and figures properly. Group participation and involvement dwindles when members react subjectively to factual data and arrive at pseudosolutions by way of hunches.

One of the greatest deterrents to good group action is that some people feel a necessity to suppress their real opinions in the interest of group harmony. Pseudoagreement results. The best, but unheard, arguments may walk out of the conference room when the meeting adjourns.

Conference leaders must learn that people will interact only when leaders respect, cherish, and recognize individual differences rather than suffocate them. Out of a climate of permissiveness and mutual appreciation, leaders can stimulate people to contribute ideas and to reach quality decisions.

• Summarize the discussion. Throughout the course of the meeting, the leader briefly reviews from time to time what has gone on before in order to bring everyone up to date. He secures a concensus and states conclusions reached and/or actions recommended.

• Make assignments, if necessary. Usually, group decisions require some sort of follow up action. The leader is responsible for making definite assignments to one or more workers to carry out the recommended actions. In most cases, the workers would receive assignments which are related to their work.

• Adjourn the group at the agreed-upon time. Any exception should have the approval of the group.

• Prepare minutes. The minutes of the meeting—the record of the things done and the decisions reached—are of prime concern to the continuing health of the staff organization. The minutes should be typed, checked by the leader, and then distributed to the conference members. Any question or correction can be submitted at the next meeting.

What is the role of the participant?

The participants in a conference are just as much responsible for the success of the meeting as is the leader. A participant engages in either group building or group blocking roles.

• Group blocking roles are as follows:

Do you arrive late?
Do you withdraw from the group when your feelings are hurt?
Do you make "off the beam" comments?
Do you dominate the discussion?
Do you impose your will on the group?
Do you tend to be arbitrary?

Do you engage in little side conferences?

Do you push for a vote or a decision before there is group agreement?

Do you tend to yield to group pressure and conform?

Do you impose your gripes on the group?

Do you communicate by your posture that you are bored?

Do you doodle?

- Group building roles are as follows:

Do you give or ask for facts?

Do you give or ask for opinions?

Do you give or ask for a solution?

Do you confine your remarks to the problem?

Do you attempt to make other members feel at ease?

Do you express yourself clearly and concisely?

Do you level (courteously) with other members?

Do you help the group stay on target?

Do you enter into the discussion?

Do you listen while another is speaking?

Do you maintain a courteous and respectful attitude to the leader as well as to the participants?

Do you keep your remarks impersonal and free from prejudice?

Do you respect the other person's point of view?

Do you assist in reaching conclusions?

Do you accept it gracefully when the decision goes against you?

Do you arrive on time and attend regularly?

How do you, the leader, evaluate the results of the meeting?

The best time to evaluate the results of the meeting is right after adjournment. You should measure your own effectiveness as a conference leader. Some questions you may ask yourself are:

Did I present the problem clearly?

Did I refer their questions to the group instead of trying to take over and answer them myself?

Did I talk too much?

Did I pull into the discussion the person who said little or nothing?

Did I stimulate their thinking?

Did I give conferees time to think?
Did I summarize clearly the thinking of the group?
Did I control distractions?
Did I give everyone an opportunity to express himself?
Did the meeting fulfill its purpose?

A probing question indeed, is to ask yourself, Do the staff members really look forward to these staff meetings?

In addition, from time to time, you may wish to "sound out" your staff on how effective staff meetings are and how to improve them. If you have already developed a participative climate with your workers, they will most likely feel free to respond openly and honestly to your request for suggestions for conference improvement.

Be sure, however, your emotional posture permits you to "take it" when suggestions are made which seem to threaten your leadership style.

What follow-up is necessary?

The real value of any meeting may not be realized until days, weeks, or even months later when the decisions reached in one or more meetings are applied to the problems, projects, program actions, or activities.

For this reason, following through on decisions agreed upon is very important. Generally, "follow through" is the most neglected area of the entire conference process. To avoid this omission, set up a program that checks, examines, prods, and guides those charged with responsibility to apply agreed-upon solutions to their work assignments.

Let it not be said of your staff meetings, "We discuss everything but never seem to settle or accomplish anything."

10
The Role of
the Personnel Committee

The personnel committee in a church is a connecting link between the paid staff and the church in matters related to personnel administration and management.

It acts mainly as a policy-making group. It usually initiates and gets church approval in areas such as employment practices, staff organization, salary plan and budgets, personnel policies and procedures, and employee benefits.

It may assist, when called upon, in counseling with the pastor on matters related to personnel and administrative problems. The members of the personnel committee do not usurp the supervisory and administrative responsibilities of the pastor or any staff person.

The pastor attends, and has a vital part in, all the meetings and deliberations of the personnel committee. Furthermore, it is his responsibility to explain the approved personnel policies and procedures to the paid staff workers and to get their acceptance.

Since the undergirding principles of Christian devotion and understanding should always be foremost in the personnel committee's ministry, it is extremely important that the church choose wisely the members to serve on this committee. Although some phases of the committee's work may seem to be technical, they can be performed well by men and women who have good judgment, are objective, and have demonstrated the ability to work well with others.

The following suggestions related to the work of the personnel committee may be applied to a church staff of any size.

Establish Employment Practices.

This responsibility includes setting up employment qualifications and skills. It also may include giving assistance to the pastor, when requested, in recruiting, interviewing, and placing the new worker on the job. The chairman of the personnel committee may take in all or part of the steps leading to the employment of a worker. Or he may assign the task to another member of the committee.

In a larger church the minister of education, business administrator, or other staff supervisor usually recruits, screens, and places on the job these workers for whom he has supervisory responsibility. Especially does this procedure apply when filling a clerical or manual vacancy.

Usually, when a church approves the addition or replacement of a professional staff worker such as minister of education, minister of music, the full personnel committee acts to assist the pastor in finding, interviewing, and recommending a qualified person for church approval.

Whatever employment procedure is used, it is desirable for the person on the church staff who is to supervise the new employee to be given an opportunity to interview the applicant and to share in the employment decision.

The personnel committee should formulate written employment policies and procedures that will serve as a guide to the staff. See chapter 1 for a more detailed review of suggested employment practices.

The pastor and the personnel committee should decide and establish the number of work hours for each day (seven, seven and one-half, eight, or more); the workday schedule (8:00 to 5:00, 8:30 to 5:30, or other); and the workweek schedule (five days, five and one-half days, or other).

Review and Update the Organization of the Staff.

Periodically, review the organization chart of the staff. The chart shows names and job titles of workers and their relationships. See chapter 3 for further information related to staff organization.

As a church grows, additional staff workers will be needed from time to time. It is the responsibility of the personnel committee to make periodic studies of the work load of the church staff to determine any necessary expansion needs.

The pastor may initiate the request for an additional worker. It is the duty of the personnel committee to review the request with him or with other supervisory staff members, then, if in order, to request church approval for action.

The addition of an office employee may require a restudy of one or more clerical job descriptions and a reassignment of some of the various job duties before a new description and job title are determined and before a new worker is employed. See chapter 4.

Likewise the addition of a professional worker may require a restudy of one or more professional position descriptions and a regrouping of duties. For example, dividing the combination job of minister of education-minister of music requires two job descriptions instead of one. The personnel committee should do its homework before prospects for the new position are recruited and screened.

The personnel committee, prior to bringing its recommendation to the church to add a new staff worker, may need to work with the budget or finance committee to determine if additional salary funds are available in this year's salary budget.

Establish a Formal Salary Plan.

The personnel committee is the logical one to initiate and set up a formal salary plan for church staff workers. The salary plan should include the professional as well as the secretarial, clerical, and manual workers. The salary of the pastor should be excluded from the formal pay grade schedules. This frees the pastor to speak for the employees in recommending salary and CPI adjustments. The personnel committee would review and authorize the granting of increases (merit and CPI) for the pastor. See chapter 5 for suggestions in establishing a formal salary plan.

The writing of a description for each position on the paid staff—regular and part time—is a requisite to setting up a salary plan. See chapter 4 for suggestions in writing job descriptions.

The personnel committee is responsible for maintaining up-to-date job descriptions, job qualifications and for reviewing periodically the salary plan and supporting policies. See chapter 5 for suggested salary policies.

The personnel committee is also responsible for making an annual study of comparable wages and salaries in the community. The committee includes in its study the percentage change in the cost of living (CPI) for the past twelve months.

This information provides the facts necessary for the personnel committee to prepare an annual budget of salary costs, including merit and CPI increases, for church approval.

Another major responsibility of the personnel committee is to review periodically the benefits provided employees by the church.

Provide Employee Benefits.

Most churches provide employee benefits—some churches more than others. Sometimes a pastor and the personnel committee learn of the need to review and upgrade the church's employee benefits when they interview a prospective professional worker. The tendency is to offer the prospective worker benefits to match those of his present position. If they exceed those of present staff members, sooner or later problems will arise. It is important for every employee to be treated fairly in the matter of employee benefits.

Most pastors desire adequate benefits for staff workers. However, he could find himself in an awkward position trying to initiate proposals if he is directly involved. Then, certainly, the need of a personnel committee is apparent. It is the logical committee to study, draft, and implement a reasonable and appropriate plan of benefits for church staff members. Such a plan should include every person paid by the church for his services. Regular part-time workers should be considered also. Exceptions might be those employees classified as temporary and those who work less than half time.

The question as to what constitutes a good plan of employee benefits often arises. Practice varies from one church to another just as the benefit plans of business establishments vary.

The personnel committee, however, should give consideration to a group of standard benefits generally included for workers. Such a group includes paid vacations, paid holidays, hospitalization, life insurance, retirement pension, sick leave, Christmas gift, paid moving expenses, housing allowance, car expense, and others. The personnel committee may wish also to consider benefits related to outside invitations received by staff members, such as revivals and educational meetings.

As the personnel committee surveys the field of possible benefits and decides which ones to include or upgrade, it also should consider whether newly included benefits will be contributory or noncontributory. A contributory benefit requires that staff members pay part of the cost. Examples might be hospitalization, life insurance, and retirement. When a new contributory benefit is added, the employees presently on the staff should be given the choice to enroll or not. After that, when new workers are added to the staff they would automatically enter the plan.

The following suggestions are steps that the personnel committee may follow in initiating a plan of benefits or in upgrading the present plan:

• Survey the benefits presently provided for staff workers by the church. The church may not have in written form statements outlining the various benefits. Or such statements may be recorded here and there in church minutes that cover several years of church action.

Seek the guidance and counsel of the pastor and other staff workers in gathering the information. Inquire as to the staff workers' interpretation of present benefits. Check the salary records to learn which paid staff members, if any, are included in a contributory or noncontributory benefit. List their names.

Prepare a graph of the findings. List the names of all staff members, including regular part-time workers on the left-hand side of the page. Across the top write in all the benefits which the church presently provides, even if some do not apply to every staff worker. Draw lines across and down the page dividing names and benefits. Place a check in the squares thus formed across the page by each name to identify benefit participation. The graph is your work sheet. See Chart 12.

• Make a survey of the benefits offered by other churches to their staff workers. Such information is especially valuable if the members of the personnel committee do not have too much information or experience in setting up a benefit plan. It is entirely possible that the results of this survey may reveal a general low level and static benefit condition. If so, the committee may wish to talk to various businessmen in the church to learn what benefits they receive or offer to their employees. After all, churches should try to maintain a competitive position in order to attract top-notch professional and office and manual workers.

• Decide on the new benefits to be included and the present benefits to be upgraded. Study each benefit separately and carefully. Seek the advice and counsel of the pastor and ask for his considered judgment in final determination.

The vacation policy, for example, may not be adequate. Perhaps

CHART 12

CHART SHOWING EMPLOYEE BENEFIT PARTICIPATION

NAME	Pension Plan		Social Security		Medical Plan		Life Insurance		Vacation	Holidays	Sick Leave with Pay	Housing Allowance	Christmas Gift	Revivals and Educational Mtgs	Parking Space	Rest Periods	(other)	(other)
	C	NC	C	NC	C	NC	C	NC										
TOTALS																		

C – Employee contributes
NC – Employee does not contribute; church pays all

one week of vacation is allowed after one year of service. The personnel committee may wish to increase the vacation time benefit for an employee to two weeks after one year of service, to three weeks for a person with five (or ten) years of service, and to four weeks for a person with fifteen (or twenty) years of service. Also the personnel committee should expand the benefit to include all staff members—custodians, maids, office workers, and others not presently covered.

Seven or eight holidays a year are usually included for workers in business establishments. A church should provide similar holiday benefits. The standard holidays are New Year's Day, Memorial Day, Independence Day, Labor Day, Thanksgiving Day, and Christmas. Some businesses give Friday after Thanksgiving Day and/or a day or a half day as Christmas Eve holiday. Other holidays which have local or state significance are sometimes included.

An important item which the personnel committee may wish to consider is group insurance that includes medical and life insurance. Local insurance companies will be glad to explain various plans and their cost.

Another important benefit is retirement pension. Most churches include the pastor, minister of education, minister of music, business administrator, and other professional staff workers in a pension plan. The personnel committee may well consider bringing all regular staff members under the same pension plan. This would be in addition to Social Security.

A church which has no pension plan or does not include all its regular workers may find it necessary, at each worker's retirement time, to make one of several subjective decisions: to do nothing; to do something; or, to be generous. The decision usually depends upon how much direct monthly expense the church at the time is able to afford. The better plan, of course, is for the church to budget pension costs annually over the work life of each employee.

Other benefits such as Christmas gift, moving expenses, sick leave, parking, housing allowance, car expense, should be given similar exploratory treatment.

• Prepare a clear and complete statement of each item to be included in the overall benefit plan. The members of the personnel committee and the pastor must agree in their understanding and interpretation of each item in the proposed total benefit plan. The best way to reach understanding is for the chairman of the personnel committee to prepare carefully written statements of each benefit, including limitations, conditions of coverage, and of the staff members to whom each shall apply. Benefits should be written in the form of church policy.

• Prepare an analysis of the cost of each benefit. When new benefits are included or present benefits upgraded, the cost to the church is usually increased. After careful study, the committee may find that the cost of desired increased benefits cannot be budgeted until the following year. Or, a longer range program covering two or more years may be considered in establishing the overall revised benefit plan. The personnel committee may find that some of the increased benefits such as vacation, holidays, or sick leave may be implemented immediately.

The course taken depends upon the cost involved. The cost is recurring year after year, and it increases as new workers are added to the staff. Also the church which presently has very few benefits may not wish to "cram its program full" the first year, even if it could afford the cost.

The personnel committee should consult with the budget committee or other church committee charged with the responsibility for reviewing new cost programs.

• The chairman of the personnel committee or member assigned presents the proposed benefit plan to the church for approval and adoption. Prepare copies for distribution at the time the proposed plan is read, explained, and recommended to the church for approval. Perhaps a summary statement of the findings of comparable benefit programs in other churches or business establishments may be helpful and informative. Be ready to give increased cost figures. With the cooperation of the budget or finance chairman, show how the increased costs can presently be absorbed, or what additional budget requirements, if any, are necessary.

• After church approval and with the assistance of the pastor, explain details of the benefit program to the paid church workers.

• Assign responsibility for the continued implementation and interpretation of benefit policies. Members of the personnel committee are not always available to discuss the benefits with new workers or to review or to interpret them to those who have served on the staff for several years. The most practical solution is for the pastor to assume this assignment as one of his administrative responsibilities. He, in turn, shares this responsibility with staff supervisors.

Copies of the benefit policies should be kept in an assigned office along with the personnel records.

• Review the benefits periodically. Perhaps every three to five years the entire benefit plan should be reviewed by the personnel committee.

Employee benefits are an accepted part of present-day economy. Salaries and benefits go together. They make up the compensation package. The benefits which a church provides its staff members are extremely important to the worker on the job as well as to the prospective worker as he considers joining the staff.

Most church members desire a good benefit program for their staff members. They usually will approve one if the matter is brought to their attention in a well-organized presentation. The personnel committee renders a significant service when it studies, drafts, recommends, and implements a reasonable and acceptable church employee benefit plan.

Prepare Personnel Policy Statements.

A policy is a guiding principle on which to base future action. A procedure is an organized grouping of statements related to a certain action that answers the questions who, what, when, and how. See Exhibits XIV and XV for sample policy and procedure formats.

A partial listing of personnel policy statements which the pastor and the personnel committee may wish to consider is as follows:

• Absence

Death in the immediate family of a worker. (One, two or more days time off? or give time off without stating days? time off with pay?)

Attendance at funerals of relatives or friends, or to serve as pall-bearer. (How much time off? one or two hours or a half day? or give time off without stating hours?)

Hospitalization and convalescence. (How much time off with pay? four, eight, twelve, or more weeks? indefinitely?)

Jury duty. (Will the worker receive full pay in addition to his jury fees? or salary minus jury fees?)

Medical appointments during work hours. (How much time without payroll deduction? one, two, or more hours on each occasion?)

Personal illness. (Time off with pay, or by some other plan?)

Personal reasons. (Time off with or without pay?)

Voting time. (Time off during the work day? Polls are usually open from seven to seven).

• Employee benefits

Accident insurance. (Cover all the employees? a few? none?)

Advance salary. (Will the church permit an employee to request his salary check before payday? If so, under what circumstances?)

Benefit status during leave of absence. (Will the church continue a worker on all benefits, some of them, or none? If some or all benefits are continued, up to how many months? If some of the benefits are contributory, will the employee on leave of absence be expected to pay his portion?)

Benefit status during military leave. (Will the benefits be continued or frozen? Usually, the insurance benefits are terminated, the pension plan frozen, and time spent in military service counted as continued church job tenure for purposes of figuring vacation eligibility and service awards).

Car expense. (For whom on the staff and how much?)

Employee training program. (Will the church encourage its paid workers to enroll in correspondence courses; night or day courses in a local school or college? If so, how much cost assistance, if any? Or will there be cost assistance if the employee takes courses at night and Saturday only?)

Group insurance—hospitalization and life. (Will the church pay all costs or employee pay part? Will all regular workers be included in the plan?)

Holidays. (Five, six, seven, or more? which holidays? When will a holiday be taken if it falls on a Saturday or a Sunday?)

Housing allowance. (How much, if any? and for whom?)

Marriage of an employee. (How much time off with pay for the honeymoon? two, three, or more days?)

Moving expenses. (For all new employees who join the staff? Will the church or the worker arrange for the carrier? Will the employee pay all costs and be reimbursed by the church? Or will the new worker submit the bill to the church for payment?)

Pension plan. (Are all employees covered? Will the church pay all costs or employees share in the cost? Or will the church pay all costs of some employees and part cost of the others?)

Physical examinations. (Should the church provide annual physical examinations for any of its workers? If so, for whom and how much cost assistance?)

Pulpit supply. (How many Sundays each year will the church be responsible for giving an honorarium to a supply preacher? How much?)

Rest periods. (One or two rest periods each work day? How much time? ten, fifteen, twenty minutes, or more, for each rest period?)

Revivals and education meetings. (How many weeks away each year? Would this benefit be extended to others as well as the pastor? If so, to whom?)

Service recognition awards. (How often? each five, ten, fifteen, twenty, years of service? Type of recognition? gift, money, or other?)

Social Security. (The local Social Security office has information outlining benefits.)

Travel insurance. (For all, part, or none of the staff? How much coverage, if any? Who pays cost?)

Vacation. (What tenure is required to be eligible for one week, two weeks, three, or more of vacation? Are all regular workers included in the plan? Will some workers have a different schedule of vacation time allowed? Must vacations be taken in units of a week or more or can an employee take a day or two at a time? Can vacations be carried over from one year to the next? Who schedules vacations of the workers?)

- Employment practices

Employment of husband and wife. (Is employment on the staff of two members of the same household acceptable?)

Employment of relatives. (Any exception? If so, what?)

Expansion of personnel. (Who initiates the request? Who approves?)

Forced termination. (For what reasons should a person be dismissed? What steps, if any, should guide the supervisor in dismissing a worker?)

Personal qualifications. (What qualifications are required for consideration for employment? age? education? experience? physical requirements? church membership?)

Reemployment of military personnel. (Refer to legal requirements.)

Reemployment of retirees. (Should you consider reemployment of church retired workers? If so, on what basis?)

Regular part-time employment. (What benefits will these employees receive, if any? On what basis will their hourly rate be figured?)

Resignation notice. (Should the church require one week's notice, two, or more, from an employee who plans to terminate? What penalty, if any, such as loss of vacation allowance, should be imposed when the employee does not give the required notice? Should any exceptions to a penalty be written into a policy?)

Screening applicants. (What requirements? use of application form? interviewing? testing? obtaining character and business references? others?)

Temporary employment. (When shall temporary employees be used? What is the length of time a temporary worker can be kept on the payroll? What is the basis for determining the hourly rate?

- Leave of absence

College or seminary study leave. (Who, if anyone, will be eligible for a quarter, semester, or more, of study? Upon what basis will eligibility be determined? tenure of service or other? Will the leave be with or without pay? If without pay, will benefits be continued?)

Military service. (Refer to the legal requirements.)

Maternity. (Get legal counsel.)

Temporary disability. (With or without pay? If with pay, for how many months? Will benefits be continued during the interim period?)

- Salary administration

Demotion of a worker. (For what reasons? Is salary adjustment involved? If so, what?)

Dismissal pay. (How much pay, if any, beyond last work day? one week? two weeks? or more? Should the dismissal paycheck include unused vacation time?)

Payroll deductions. (What items will be deducted from salary checks?)

Promotion to a higher job. (On what basis will the salary be determined? promotability? how processed?)

Salary increases. (On what basis will salaries of employees be increased? automatic? every January? based on tenure of service? based on job performance? Can an employee's salary be increased more than one step at a time?)

- Miscellaneous

Garnishments. (Get legal counsel.)

Membership in professional, civic, and service organizations. (Will the church pay all, part, or none of the cost? If all or part of the cost is paid by the church, who on the staff is eligible to participate?)

Parking. (Will special places be assigned to all or only to part of the paid staff workers during the work week? on Sunday?)

Personnel records. (What records, if any, will be set up? application file? individual salary records? pension and group insurance records? Who will maintain the rcords?)

Workday schedule. (How many hours a day? What are the starting and closing times?)

Workweek schedule. (How many days a week? five? five and one-half days or more? staggered schedule on Saturday?)

Formalized personnel policies and procedures, which are carefully considered and tailored to fit the needs of a church, almost eliminate the necessity for making decisions each time an emergency situation arises. In making these provisions, the personnel committee frees the pastor and his staff to perform their tasks more effectively and efficiently.

Prepare a Church-Staff Administration Handbook.

The purpose of this section is to suggest guidelines for your use in preparing your own church-staff administration handbook.

Some of the suggested items to include may not be appropriate or applicable to your church's needs. Other items not suggested may be more suitable and timely for your own tailored handbook.

What is the purpose of a church-staff administration handbook?

The handbook's main purpose is to communicate clearly to all church members including staff workers the church's plan of internal administration.

The handbook serves these needs:

• For use when conducting orientation sessions for new church members. A copy of the handbook should be provided each new member.

• For use by church members. It is amazing indeed how uninformed many members are of the various internal operations of their church. Not a few members would respond "I don't know" to questions such as "Does your church have a written constitution

CHURCH STAFF ADMINISTRATION

and bylaws?" Do you have a church council? Who can use the chapel for weddings? Can a member borrow chairs, dishes, and so forth, for use at his home for a class party? Can a teacher borrow the church bus to take his class members to the park for a picnic? Does our church sponsor a mission?

• For use by the paid staff workers. A handbook reduces considerably the need for interoffice communication. Its use facilitates the handling of inquiries which come from outside the church.

• For use by the prospective professional staff worker prior to his coming for an interview. The handbook answers for him a number of questions about how your church operates. The resulting interviewing process is greatly enhanced.

What items might be considered for a church-staff handbook?

The handbook divides logically into two sections: items related to the administration of the church and items related to the administration of the church staff.

As you read the following list of entries in the table of contents, you will come to one conclusion: you already have much of the material hidden in several sets of church minutes, documents or records.

Introduction (prepared by the pastor):
Our Church:
    The Purpose of Our Church
    The History of Our Church
    Our Church Constitution and Bylaws
    The Program Organizations of Our Church
    The Deacon Body
    The Church Council
    Our Church Officers and Their Responsibilities
    Our Church Committees and Their Responsibilities
    Our Church Budget
    Activities Sponsored by Our Church
    Missions Sponsored by Our Church
    The Policies of Our Church
    The Services of Our Church
Our Paid Staff:
    The Purpose of Our Church Staff
    The Organization of Our Staff

Church Staff Job Descriptions
Church Staff Salary Plan and Administration
Policies Covering Staff Personnel
Employee Benefits
Staff Meetings
Employee Services
Health and Safety

Who prepares the material for a church-staff handbook?

The church council and the personnel committee are the logical groups to work together in producing the handbook.

The church council members assume the responsibility for preparing materials listed under "Our Church" section of the handbook.

The personnel committee members assume the responsibility for preparing materials listed under the "Our Paid Staff" section of the handbook.

A subcommittee comprised of members of both groups is one way to coordinate the preparation, publication, and distribution of the handbook.

If the cooperative agreement does not materialize, the personnel committee should proceed with the publication of the "Our Paid Staff" section of the handbook.

As indicated earlier, some of the material suitable for the handbook is stored in several different sets of church records. This material should be scrutinized as to its relevance. Some items should be revised, rewritten or updated while other items should be created.

Church-Related items for the handbook may include:

1. *A statement of "the purpose of our church."*
Several differently stated paragraphs defining the church's purpose are given here. Perhaps one of these is compatible with your concept of the purpose of your church. Or perhaps an idea or suggestion in one or more paragraphs will be helpful as you prepare your own statement of the purpose of your church.

• The continuing purpose of our church is to share Christ with the whole world; to develop mature Christians and to apply Christian principles in all of life's relationships through worship, witness, education, and ministry.

• The purpose of our church is to represent God to man and man to God. Each believer is a priest. He should confront men with the claims of Christ; he should also try to help men in this confrontation to find a satisfying and saving relationship with Christ. This purpose should hold for all members of our church.

• The purpose of our church is to provide a fellowship of believers in Christ as his family of redeemed who are united to carry out his will. Our church has the commands of Christ in the Great Commission and in the work outlined in the New Testament. Our church is to relate to the spiritual needs of the community through ministries it performs. Our church has the larger outreach through the world and cooperates with other churches of like faith and order in carrying out God's work in the association, state, nation, and around the world.

• The purpose of our church is to

Make available worship opportunities by providing leadership, appropriate accommodations, and facilities

Provide a program of religious education majoring on Bible study and emphasizing the implications of the Christian life

Cultivate leadership to carry out the church's God-given tasks

Encourage true fellowship *(koinonia)* among its members by fostering a mutual spirit of active concern

Proclaim the gospel by group and individual acts of witness so that the unsaved may be won to faith in Christ and enlisted in church membership

Engage in missions to share the church's ministry and message with an ever-widening constituency throughout the world.

2. *A brief history of our church.*

You may already have a written history of your church. If so, you may wish to condense it to two or three pages for inclusion in your handbook. If you do not have a written church history or if you have a copy that needs updating, the following outline may help.

1. Background and beginnings
2. Chronological development—pastors, locations, buildings, and so forth
3. Educational growth and development
4. Ministries, activities, missions
5. Growth of church staff
6. Outstanding leaders

7. Chart showing record of past ten years: church membership; enrollment in church program organizations; annual budget figures and receipts; and so forth

3. *Our church's constitution and bylaws.*
What to include in the constitution:

A preamble, setting forth the purpose of the constitution
The name of the church—its official legal title
The objectives (purpose) of the church
The church doctrinal statement or Articles of Faith
Relationships—a statement of the church's relationships to other groups
Church covenant

What to include in the bylaws:

Membership: qualifications for church members and how they may be received; voting rights of church members; termination of membership; discipline; new member orientation; and member restoration
General church officers
    (1) Pastor—call, duties, termination
    (2) Other staff members—selection, duties, termination
    (3) Deacons—number, election, term, duties, meetings
    (4) Moderator—selection, duties
    (5) Clerk—selection, duties
    (6) Treasurer—selection, duties
    (7) Trustees—selection, duties
    (8) Other needed officers
Church committees
Program services (recreation and library)—selection, duties
Program organizations (Sunday School, Church Training, Woman's Missionary Union, Brotherhood, Church Music)—purpose, officers, election
Ordinances—preparation for, conducting
Church meetings
    (1) Worship—Sunday, Wednesday, other
    (2) Special services—revivals, study courses, clinics, and so forth
    (3) Business meetings—regular and special

(4) Quorum
(5) Parliamentary rules
Church finances—budget, accounting, and so forth
Church operations manual
Amendments

How much detail should we include in presenting the program organization of our church?

Several different approaches may be considered in presenting your church's program organizations. Keep in mind that the more detailed the information, the more quickly the information becomes obsolete.

• Name the program organizations—Sunday School, Church Training, Church Music, Woman's Missionary Union, and Brotherhood—without giving any additional information.

• Or show a detailed organization chart of each program without the names of the directors, teachers, leaders, and so forth.

• Or state the principal function and tasks of each program. This information is available in the program organization administration study books.

• Or give statistical information covering the past five to ten years of program enrollment, average attendance, number of departments and classes.

• Or include a combination of one or more of the above.

Is it necessary to repeat an item in the handbook already included in the church's constitution and bylaws?

No. Information about the deacons, for example, may be amply covered in the constitution and bylaws. The same might apply to church officers, church committees, and so forth.

What church committees are usually included in a church's roster of committees?

The list below is not all-inclusive. Some churches have fewer than fifteen church committees while other churches have twenty or more. It depends upon the need. The need for fewer or more committees may change from time to time. Since a church is dynamic and not static, its statements of internal administration should not be "locked in" to preclude meeting quickly changing situations.

The names of the committees are as follows:

Baptism	Food services	Property and space
Bereavement	History	Public relations
Budget planning	Internationals	Special events
Bus	Kindergarten	Stewardship
Church membership	Long-Range planning	Systems control
Church nominating	Lord's Supper preparation	Ushers
Elevator	Ministries	Wills and endowment
Finance	Missions	Youth
Flower	Personnel	

What is a sample format of a church committee duty description?

Nominating Committee

Principal Function: The nominating committee is responsible to the church for leading in staffing all church elected offices and church committees and for assisting program directors in staffing their program organizations.

Membership: The nominating committee shall be composed of twelve members. (Some nominating committees have three, six, or nine members depending on the size of the church.) One third of the members shall rotate each year. A member may be reelected after one year's absence from the committee.

Program organization directors may be co-opted to serve as ex officio members. The chairman of the nominating committee will consult with the pastor on all nominees before names are presented to the church for election.

Duties:

1. Develop a plan to discover the manpower resources to give leadership to all church elected places of leadership.

2. Establish a calendar for the selection, election, and training of all persons to fill church elected positions.

3. Work with church program leaders to clear all names of prospective workers before contact to make sure a person is being considered for only one job at a time.

4. Evaluate all requests for leadership needs; distribute church leadership according to priority needs of the church.

5. Select prospective workers to fill all positions and assign responsibility for interviewing and enlisting the person by a member of the nominating committee prior to recommendation to the church.

6. Nominate special committees as authorized by the church. Prepare duties for new committees prior to leadership selection and election.

7. Review periodically the duties of church committees to determine their continued need or revision of duties.

8. Recommend the deletion and/or addition of such committees as may be needed to accomplish the work of the church.

9. Engage in a year-round vigilance to maintain a full complement of workers in all church-elected positions.

10. Present names of nominees to the church for election.

What are the purpose, function, and duties of a church council?

Here are several paragraphs that may be helpful.

Purpose: The purpose of the church council is to assist our church in planning, coordinating, and evaluating its overall programs and services. The church council is an advisory and correlating agent through which all church organizations and committees may coordinate their activities into one harmonious effort.

Principal Function: To assist the church in determining its course and to coordinate its work.

Method of Election: Church leaders become members of the church council by virtue of their church leadership position.

Membership: Pastor (chairman); church staff members, such as minister of education, minister of music; directors of the church education organization; and chairman of deacons. Other members may include the director of library services, the recreation director, church committee chairmen, and church officers. Ex officio members are expected to attend when matters relating to their work are to be discussed.

Term of office: Term corresponds to the term in church-elected position.

Frequency of meetings: Monthly, and more often if needed.

Officers: Chairman, vice-chairman, secretary. The vice-chairman and secretary are appointed by the chairman.

Reporting: The church council reports to the church.

Duties of council members:

1. Lead the church to state its purpose and objectives.

2. Initiate and coordinate activities to discover church and community needs.

3. Formulate and recommend to the church a plan of work for one to three years.

4. Review and coordinate activities of church programs and services.

5. Evaluate program achievements and report regularly to the church.

What other items may be included in the church section of the handbook?

• The annual church budget. Include a copy of the most recent annual budget. Although the budget figures will be obsolete within a year, the identification of budgeted objects will provide useful information.

• Activities sponsored by the church. Perhaps your church sponsors activities such as Scouts of America, literacy classes, English classes for internationals, kindergarten, mother's day out, and so forth. If so, list each activity separately giving information about meeting place, time schedule, and so forth.

• Missions sponsored by the church. Identify each mission separately giving information such as history, location, facilities, programs, activities, growth, and potential outreach.

• Church policies. Include policy statements related to matters affecting church members such as

Use of church property and equipment

Use of church library

Use of church organ

• Schedule of services and meetings. Include a time schedule of the regular Sunday and Wednesday educational organization meetings and worship services. Refer to seasonal changes, if any. Include other regular meetings such as weekly workers' meeting, fellowship supper, visitation day, and so forth.

Staff-Related Items for the Handbook

What items are appropriate to include in the staff section of the handbook?

• The purpose of our church staff.

Several paragraphs defining the purpose of a church staff are given here. Perhaps one of these is compatible with your concept of a staff. Or perhaps an idea or suggestion in one or more paragraphs will be helpful as you prepare your own statement of purpose.

1. The purpose of our church staff is to lead the church in accomplishing its mission of proclaiming the gospel to believers and unbelievers and caring for the church's members and for other persons in the community.

2. The purpose of our church staff is to provide inspiration, guidance, and opportunities for church members to fulfill their priestly role. This involves proclaiming the gospel, teaching, training, witnessing, planning, and scheduling actions to achieve the church's mission. Our church staff should be sufficiently involved in doing the work to enable them to function effectively in directing the work. They should serve as enablers or equippers to get every member ready and willing to carry out his respective responsibilities.

3. The purpose of our church paid staff is to plan and administer the programs of work of the church; to plan adequate organization according to the need; to enlist and train leadership for the various places of responsibility; and to stimulate and challenge the church to action in supporting and carrying out the designed programs of work.

• The organization of your church staff. As an introduction, you may wish first to state the purpose and advantages of good organization followed by a chart showing the organization of your church paid staff. See chapter 3.

• Church staff job descriptions. Include a complete set of job descriptions covering the work of every employee on the staff—regular and regular part-time.

Refer to chapter 4 for suggestions on how to write descriptions and the Appendix for sample copies of church staff descriptions.

• Church staff salary plan. See chapter 5 for suggestions in establishing and administering a formal salary plan.

• Policies covering staff personnel. See the section in this chapter under the title, "Prepare Personnel Policy Statements," for a suggested list of policy statements.

• Church staff work policies and procedures. See exhibits XIV and XV in the Appendix section for suggested format.

• Employee benefits. Include statements or paragraphs covering the various benefits—eligibility, cost, and so forth.

• Staff meetings. Give information as to the day and time of regularly scheduled staff meetings. See chapter 9 for helpful suggestions in planning and conducting staff meetings.

• Health and safety. Include the following information: Location of the first aid kit; locations and directions for use of fire extinguishers; police, fire, doctor, and ambulance telephone numbers; fire evacuation plan for paid staff; building security plan; to whom to report work hazards; the importance of maintaining an orderly work place; workman's compensation, and so forth.

The church-staff handbook can be produced economically. Ask a qualified member of your church to read the first draft of all the material. Check for spelling, grammar, sentence structure, paragraphing, and clarity.

Enlist volunteer workers to type the final copy. They should follow a format design so all pages will have order and system. Number the pages consecutively. Include a contents page.

Duplicate the material on the church's duplicating machine. Ask volunteers to help collate the pages. Purchase heavier paper stock for the front and back cover and bind the handbooks. The front cover should identify the handbook by title, church, and year. Give the "home produced" handbook as much class as possible. It should be neat and attractive.

Periodically, throughout the time span of preparing materials, keep the members informed of interesting progress reports through the columns of your church bulletin. This type of communication will add to the reading interest of members after the handbooks are distributed to them.

"Putting out" a handbook is a lot of work. But it's worth it.

Exhibits and
Sample Job Descriptions

EXHIBIT I

APPLICATION FORM (Sample)

(for secretarial, clerical, manual jobs)
_____Church

Date_____

I. PERSONAL DATA

Name (last)_____(first)_____(middle)_____
Address(street)_____
  (city)_____(state)_____(zip code)_____
Phone Number_____(Social Security Number)_____
Birth Date (month)_____(day)_____(year)_____
Marital Status: Single__ Married__ Divorced__ Separated__ Widow__

II. EDUCATION

High School Diploma: yes____ no____; if yes, when?_____
Business College: yes____ no____; if yes, where located?_____
University or College: yes__ no__; if yes, did you graduate?____
  What was your major?_____Minor?_____
  Name and location of college_____
Seminary: yes____ no____; if yes, did you graduate?_____
  Degree_____Where is Seminary located?_____
School or college activities in which you engaged?_____

III. EMPLOYMENT HISTORY (Start with present or most recent job)

1. Name of Employer_____
   Address_____
   Worked from_____to_____Monthly·salary or hourly rate_____
   Type of work performed_____
   Reason for leaving_____

2. Name of Employer_____
   Address_____
   Worked from_____to_____Monthly salary or hourly rate_____
   Reason for leaving_____

3. Name of Employer_____
   Address_____
   Worked from_____to_____Monthly salary or hourly rate_____
   Reason for leaving_____

(Please complete page 2)

EXHIBIT I

APPLICATION FORM (Sample)
(Page 2)

IV. JOB DATA (Check areas in which you have had experience or training)

___Typing (Speed___WPM)   ___Receptionist
___Shorthand (Speed___WPM)   ___Writing and Editing
___Transcribing Machine   ___Supervisor
___Bookkeeping   ___Custodian
___Duplicating Machine
___Addressograph Machine

V. CHURCH LIFE

Denomination_____
Name of Church (Where you hold membership)_____
  Location_____
  What church activities did (do) you participate in?_____

VI. HEALTH

How would you describe your general health?_____
Hearing?_____Eyesight?_____
Physical defects, if any?_____
Date of last physical examination_____

VII. CHARACTER REFERENCES (Do not list relatives or former employers)

1. Name_____Address_____
   Occupation_____Years Known_____

2. Name_____Address_____
   Occupation_____Years Known_____

3. Name_____Address_____
   Occupation_____Years Known_____

VIII. ADDITIONAL INFORMATION

Please give us any additional information you desire about your education and experience (Include any special talents)

Please Sign Your Name_____

EXHIBIT 1 A

PERSONAL DATA SHEET   (Sample)

(for professional positions)

Date_____

I. PERSONAL DATA

Name (last)_____(first)_____(middle)_____

Birth Date (month)_____(day)_____(year)_____

Social Security Number_____

Marital status_____Name of spouse_____No. of children_____

II. EDUCATION

High School Diploma: yes___ no___; If yes, when?_____
Business College: Yes___ no___; if yes, where located?_____
University or college: yes___ no___; if yes, did you graduate?_____
     What was your major?_____Minor_____
     Name and location of college_____
Seminary: yes___ no___; if yes, did you graduate?_____
     Degree_____Where is Seminary located_____
School or college activities in which you engaged_____
_____

III. EMPLOYMENT HISTORY (Start with present or most recent position)
1.
Name of church or employer_____
Address_____
In this position from _____to_____Annual salary_____

2.
Name of church or employer_____
Address_____
In this position from_____to_____Annual salary_____

3.
Name of church or employer_____
Address_____
In this position from_____to_____Annual salary_____

EXHIBIT II

TELEPHONE QUESTIONNAIRE

(Business Reference Guide)

Applicant's Name_____Address_____

Call made to_____of_____Phone_____
(Company)

1. Verify dates of employment: From_____to_____

2. Was he under your supervision?_____If no, under whom?_____

3. What was his position in your firm?_____

4. How would you rate his performance in that position?
   Above average____; Average____; Below average____

5. Why did he leave your employ?_____

6. Could he have advanced if he had stayed with you?_____
   If so, to what type of work?_____

7. We are considering him for _____job. Do you think he can perform
   this type work?_____

8. How did he get along with his superiors? Well____Fairly well_____
   Poorly____

9. How did he get along with other workers? Well____Fairly well_____
   Poorly____

10. Was he dependable?____

11. Was he regular in attendance and punctual?_____

12. Would you rehire him if circumstances permitted?_____

13. To your knowledge does he have any undesirable habits?_____
    Speech___; Dress___; Personal hygiene___; Other_____

14. What are his strongest traits?_____
    Weakest_____

15. Is there any comment you would like to add which has not been
    discussed?_____

16. Verify, if possible, the position and title of the person called

17. Person called was: Cooperative_____ Uncooperative_____
                       Pleasant_____ Unpleasant_____
                       Knew facts_____ Hesitated_____
                       Willing to help_____ Unwilling_____

Call made by_____Date_____

EXHIBIT III

TELEPHONE QUESTIONNAIRE

(Character Reference Guide)

(Page 2)

Applicant's Name_____Address_____

Call made to_____Telephone_____

Give some idea of the job for which applicant is being considered.

1. How long have you known the applicant?_____

2. Are you a friend of the family?_____A school friend_____
    Through what source did you meet the applicant?_____

3. How does he spend his spare time? Sports?_____Reading?_____
    Hobby?_____Other?_____

4. Does he have many or few friends?_____

5   How does he get along with them?_____

6. We understand he is a member of the_____Church
    Does he attend regularly?_____What does he do in church work?

7. To your knowledge does he have any undesirable habits?_____
    Speech_____; Dress_____; Personal hygiene_____; Other_____

8. What are his strongest traits?_____
    Weakest?_____

9. Is there any comment you would like to add which has not been
    discussed?_____

10. Person called was: Cooperative_____ Uncooperative_____
                        Pleasant_____ Unpleasant_____
                        Knew facts_____ Hesitated_____
                        Willing to help_____ Unwilling_____

Call made by_____Date_____

EXHIBIT IV

CHARACTER REFERENCE INQUIRY

Please return to_____Church

(Address)_____

(Person's name who will receive this information)_____

TO:_____

ADDRESS:_____DATE_____

NAME OF APPLICANT:_____AGE_____

The applicant whose name appears above has made application with
us for employment. Please give us information requested below
any any additional comment. Information will be kept confidential.

1. How long have you known the applicant?_____
2. Are you a friend of the family?_____

Please rate the applicant

QUALIFICATIONS	EXCELLENT	GOOD	FAIR	POOR	DO NOT KNOW
Moral conduct					
Work attitude					
Ability to get along with others					
Dependability					
Honesty					
Personal habits					
Physical health					

Additional comments:

SIGNED_____DATE_____

EXHIBIT V

BUSINESS REFERENCE INQUIRY

Please return to_____Church

(Address)_____

(Person's name who will receive this information)_____

_____

TO: _____

ADDRESS:_____DATE_____

NAME OF APPLICANT_____AGE_____

The applicant whose name appears above has made application with us for employment. Please give us the information requested below and any additional comments. Information will be kept confidential.

1. Claims employment with you as _____yes____no_____
2. Worked with you from _____ to_____yes_____no_____
3. Was actually employed as_____
4. At a beginning salary of_____closing salary of_____
5. Was laid off_____discharged_____left voluntarily_____
6. Would you reemploy? yes_____no_____ If not, please give reason
_____

7. Please rate the applicant

QUALIFICATIONS	EXCELLENT	GOOD	FAIR	POOR	DO NOT KNOW
Physical health					
Job competence					
Dependability					
Ability to get along with others					
Work attitude					
Personal habits					
Record of attendance and punctuality					

8. Additional Comments:

SIGNED_____DATE_____

POSITION_____

EXHIBIT V1

CHURCH STAFF ORGANIZATION CHARTS (8 Samples)

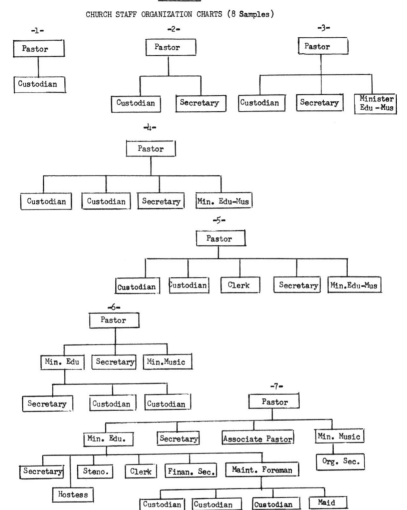

EXHIBIT VI A

- 8 -

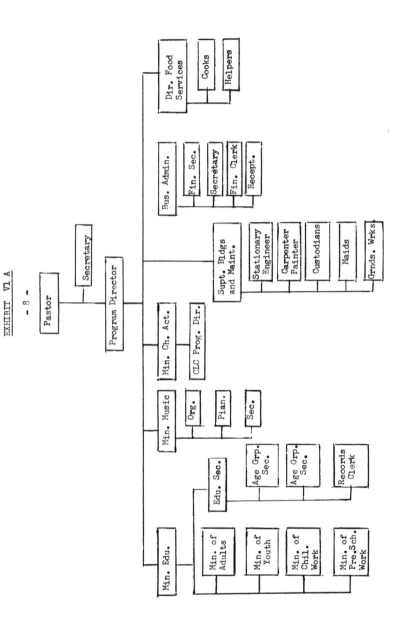

EXHIBIT VII

POSITION QUESTIONNAIRE FORM

(Secretarial-Clerical-Manual)

_____Church

Present Job Title_____Date_____

Name of Supervisor_____Prepared by_____

1. PRINCIPAL FUNCTION:

2. REGULAR DUTIES: (List the major duties that your job   Approx. amount
                    normally requires you to perform)   of time on each
                                                                task

3. OTHER DUTIES: (List the duties you perform that are not on a
                  regular basis)

(Please complete page 2)

EXHIBIT VII

POSITION QUESTIONNAIRE FORM

(Secretarial-Clerical-Manual)

(page 2)

The following questions are intended to clarify the special skills, knowledge, and experience required to fulfil the normal requirements of the job.

4. WHAT KIND OF OFFICE EQUIPMENT DO YOU USE?

(Machine or Equipment)   (Used occasionally, frequently, continuously)

5. WHAT SKILLS DOES THIS JOB REQUIRE?   (Such as typing, shorthand, proofreading, filing, etc.)

6. DOES THIS JOB REQUIRE

    (1) assigning routine work to others?_____
    (2) or, giving direct supervision to others?_____
         List names of those directly supervised, if any_____

7. WHAT DECISIONS DO YOU NORMALLY MAKE IN THIS POSITION WITHOUT ·GETTING APPROVAL?

(Nature of the Decision)   (Frequency of Occurrence)

8. WHAT CONTACTS DO YOU MAKE WITH PEOPLE OUTSIDE THE CHURCH?

(Printers, vendors, etc.)

9. ADDITIONAL COMMENTS   (Which will help to describe your job completely

10. PLEASE WRITE WHAT YOU CONSIDER IS THE MAIN PURPOSE OF YOUR JOB

EXHIBIT VIII

POSITION DESCRIPTION FORM

(Secretarial-Clerical-Manual)

_____Church

Job Title_____Date_____

1. <u>PRINCIPAL FUNCTION</u>:

2. <u>REGULAR DUTIES</u>:

3. <u>OTHER DUTIES</u>:

4. <u>REQUIRED JOB QUALIFICATIONS</u>:

       Education
       Experience
       Skills

EXHIBIT IX

PROFESSIONAL—SUPERVISORY POSITION QUESTIONNAIRE

Church	Prepared by	Date

This Questionnaire is intended to assist you in describing completely the job under consideration. Please read all of the Questionnaire carefully before writing anything. Make sure your answers are informative and complete. Use additional sheets if necessary.

1. Please state briefly the purpose of the job.

2. List the specialized knowledge obtained through education and experience this job requires.

SPECIALIZED KNOWLEDGE	LENGTH OF TIME

3. List the activities this job normally requires, estimating the percentage of time required for each.

ACTIVITY	PERCENT OF TIME

4. List the activities this job sometimes requires, but not on a routine or regularly assigned basis.

	FREQUENCY OF OCCURRENCE

(Please complete page 2)

EXHIBIT IX

(page 2)   PROFESSIONAL-SUPERVISORY POSITION QUESTIONAIRE

5. List examples of programs and/or projects for which this job provides leadership.

6. List the more important decisions the job normally requires without review by higher authority.

Nature of Decision	Frequency of Occurrence

7. List the type of decisions the job normally requires but with review and/or approval by higher authority.

Nature of Decision	Frequency of Occurrence

8. List all professional people reporting directly to this position.

Name	Title

9. List all secretarial, clerical, manual persons supervised on this job not included in the above category.

Job Title	Number of Employees

10. On what matters, if any, is the church represented by the employee in his relationships with groups or persons not employed by the church.

EXHIBIT X
(Professional-Supervisory)
POSITION DESCRIPTION FORM

Job Title   Reports to

PRINCIPAL FUNCTION

RESPONSIBILITIES

SPECIFICATIONS (MINIMUM REQUIREMENTS)
Education
Experience
Date Evaluated

SALARY CONTROL RECORD

EXHIBIT XI

Name (Last) _____ (First) _____ (Initial) _____ Employment Date _____ Birthday _____

EFF. DATE	JOB TITLE	PAY GRA.	SALARY	ADJ. CODE	% OF INC.	$ INC.	ANNIV. MO.

ADJ. CODES:
A—MERIT INCREASE
B—STRUCTURE INCREASE
C—PROMOTION
D—DEMOTION
E—TO BASE INCREASE
F—OTHER

EXHIBIT XII

JOB RESULTS EVALUATION

Professional-Supervisory Employees

Instructions: Supervisor complete in triplicate prior to scheduled meeting with employee. Retain original; duplicate to employee and triplicate to next upward level of supervision, if any.

Employee _____ Job Title _____ Date _____

Completed by Supervisor

Effectiveness of Goal (Tasks) Accomplishment
(Evaluate the level of employee attainment-performance)

	Below Satisfactory Level	Satisfactory Level	Surpasses Satisfactory Level	Far Exceeds Satisfactory Level
1. Concept and grasp of the job				
2. Timeliness of goals				
3. Quality of the planning process				
4. Quantity of acceptable work				
5. Promptness of reports				
6. Effectiveness of overall work goal (task) achievement				
7. Self-improvement goal accomplishment				

8. In what work area(s), if any, does this employee need help and/or to improve?
9. In what leadership skill(s), if any, does this worker need to improve?
10. What additional work goals would you suggest to this worker for his/her consideration at the next planning cycle?
11. What additional self-improvement goals would you suggest to this worker for his/her consideration at the next planning cycle?

_____ Signature of Supervisor _____ Date

EXHIBIT XII A

SUMMARY OF RESULTS APPROACH

Job Performance Review
Professional-Supervisory

Instructions: Supervisor requests employee
to complete this form in duplicate prior to
job performance meeting date. The employee
gives duplicate copy to supervisor at meeting; both bring goal detail to meeting.

Employee _____ Job Title _____ Date _____

Completed by Employee

1. In which goal(s) or task assignments (write them) do you feel you are making your most
significant contribution? Why?

2. In which goal(s) or task assignments (write them) do you feel you are not satisfied
with your progress? Why?

3. What problems or difficulties, if any, did you encounter in goal attainment?

4. In what ways could your supervisor be of greater assistance in helping you attain your
goals?

5. On what tasks, duties, etc., have you spent most of your time during the past six
months?

6. What do you feel is the single biggest problem you face in the performance of your job?

   (1) Over which you have control?

   (2) Which is outside your control?

7. What progress are you making in your self-improvement goals?

8. What (additional) work goals do you suggest for the next planning cycle?

9. What (additional) self-improvement goals do you suggest for the next planning cycle?

EXHIBIT XIII

JOB PERFORMANCE EVALUATION

Secretarial–Clerical–Manual

Instruction: Supervisor completes in triplicate: He keeps original and gives duplicate to employee. Both copies brought to scheduled meeting. Triplicate copy to next upward level of supervision.

Employee	Job Title	Date
	Completed by Supervisor	

1. Based on this person's job description and your observation of the work produced by this employee which skills listed below are engaged in?

Receptionist	Shorthand	Editing	Custodial
Typing	Transcriptionist	Layout	Machine repair
Filing	Grammar	Art work	Painting
Human Relations	Spelling	Key Punch	Furniture repair
Communications	Punctuation	P B X	Carpentry
Other (Name)	Other (Name)	Other (Name)	Equipment operator

2. In which skills checked do you feel this employee excels?

3. In which skills checked do you feel this employee needs to improve?

4. What improvement plans, if any, were agreed upon in the performance review session?

(Please complete page 2)

EXHIBIT XIII

(Page 2)

9. How would you rate this employee's performance on the job in the following areas? Place a check in the space you feel is appropriate.

	Below Satisfactory Level	Satisfactory Level	Surpasses Satisfactory Level	Far Exceeds Satisfactory Level
1. Work Skills Ability				
	(Refers to the effective application of work skills required.)			
2. Quantity of Work				
	(How much acceptable work is produced in a given time)			
3. Quality of Work				
	(How thorough, accurate and acceptable is the work performed)			
4. Work Relationships				
	(How cooperative and how well he/she works as a team member)			
5. Work Habits				
	(Refers to initiative, dependability, attendance, punctuality, manner of work)			
6. Innovation				
	(Refers to new ideas, systems, and methods)			
7. Self-improvement Progress				
	(Refers to extent a person improves him/herself for greater work performance)			

Signature of Supervisor   Date

EXHIBIT XIII A

JOB PERFORMANCE EVALUATION

Instruction: Employee completes in duplicate: keeps original for use in scheduled meeting; gives duplicate to supervisor at the meeting.

Secretarial–Clerical–Manual

Employee	Job Title	Date

Completed by Employee

1. Based on your job description and work assignments, what work skills are required for you to perform your overall job successfully? **Please Check.**

Receptionist	Shorthand	Editing	Custodial
Typing	Transcriptionist	Layout	Machine repair
Filing	Grammar	Art work	Painting
Human Relations	Spelling	Key Punch	Furniture repair
Communications	Punctuation	P B X	Carpentry
Other (Name)	Other (Name)	Other (Name)	Equipment operator

2. In which of the work skills you have checked do you feel you excel?

3. In which of the work skills you have checked do you feel you need to improve, if any?

4. What improvement plan do you propose?

5. What frustrations, if any, do you encounter in performing your job?

6. In what ways, if any, could your supervisor be of greater help to you in the performance of your job?

7. On what tasks, duties, have you spent most of your time during the past six months?

8. Do you have any comments, suggestions on work improvements, or whatever that you would like to discuss with your supervisor?

(Please complete page 2)

Exhibit XIII A

(Page 2)

9. How would you rate your performance on the job in the following areas?
Place a check in the space you feel is appropriate.

		Below Satisfactory Level	Satisfactory Level	Surpasses Satisfactory Level	Far Exceeds Satisfactory Level
1.	Work Skills Ability		(Refers to the effective application of work skills required.)		
2.	Quantity of Work		(How much acceptable work is produced in a given time)		
3.	Quality of Work		(How thorough, accurate and acceptable is the work performed)		
4.	Work Relationships		(How cooperative and how well you work as a team member)		
5.	Work Habits		Refers to your initiative, dependability, attendance, punctuality, manner of work)		
6.	Innovation		(Refers to new ideas, systems, and methods)		
7.	Self-improve- ment Progress		(Refers to extent you improve yourself for greater work performance)		

EXHIBIT XIV

POLICY

(Suggested Format)

SUBJECT: Vacation policy (example only)

PURPOSE: To establish policy concerning vacations for regular
            employees

POLICY:

1. One week is granted after six months of continuous
   service and a second week after completing twelve
   months of continuous service. Both weeks may be
   taken as a unit after completing twelve months of
   continuous service.

2. Employees who have completed ten years of service are
   eligible for three weeks of vacation.

3. Employees who have completed twenty years of service
   are eligible for four weeks of vacation.

4. The pastor shall be entitled to four weeks of vacation each year.

5. The pastor and other staff supervisors shall by January
   1 arrange vacation schedules so that time off will not
   seriously handicap the work or require employment of
   temporary workers except in extreme emergencies.

6. The vacation is considered as being applicable to
   and for the calendar year.

7. An employee may have an additional week of vacation
   without pay upon the pastor's approval.

8. Paid holidays which occur during the employee's vacation are to be added to the beginning or end of the vacation period.

9. Vacation periods may be divided but not less than units of one week.

10. Vacation time is not accumulative from one year to the next; nor can an employee use vacation time in a current year that would be earned in the following year.

11. Employees will not receive additional pay for a vacation not taken.

12. When at least two weeks' notice of termination is given, the employee will receive vacation allowance pay for onehalf of unused vacation if termination occurs before July 1 and full allowance pay if termination occurs July 1 or later.

13. Any deviation from this policy must be approved by the most immediate supervisor and the pastor.

EXHIBIT XV

PROCEDURE
(Suggested Format)

SUBJECT: Weekly Bulletin--Publishing the (Example only)

PURPOSE: To guide employees in publishing the bulletin

PROCEDURE:

Professional workers

1. Prepare copy and place on desk of pastor's secretary by 1:00 each Monday afternoon.

Pastor's Secretary (or other)

2. Edit copy; type according to printing specifications; mark type and prepare layout.

3. Work with professional staff to enlarge, change, or cut copy to fit space.

4. Place completed copy and layout on pastor's desk by 8:00 A.M. Tuesday.

Pastor

5. Check copy and layout; upon approval return to secretary's desk by noon Tuesday.

Pastor's Secretary

6. Deliver copy to printer by 1:00 P.M. Tuesday for Thursday noon delivery.

7. Distribute one copy to each staff member and file five copies.

8. Deliver remaining copies to clerk-typist's desk by 2:00 P.M. Thursday.

Clerk-typist

9. Operate the addressing machine; stuff, seal, stamp, and tie the envelopes for mailing.

10. Give to church custodian by 4:30 P.M. Thursday for delivery to the post office.

Custodian

11. Deliver bulletins to post office before 5:00 P.M. Thursday.

PASTOR

PRINCIPAL FUNCTION:

The pastor is responsible to the _____Church
for proclamation of the gospel of Jesus Christ, to teach the Biblical
revelation, to engage in pastoral care ministries, to provide administrative leadership in all areas of church life and to act as the
chief administrator of the paid staff.

RESPONSIBILITIES:

1. Plan and conduct the worship services; prepare and deliver sermons;
   lead in observance of ordinances.

2. Lead the church in an effective program of witnessing and in a
   caring ministry for persons in the church and community.

3. Visit members and prospects.

4. Conduct counseling sessions; perform wedding ceremonies;
   conduct funerals.

5. Serve as chairman of the church council to lead in planning,
   organizing, directing, coordinating, and evaluating the total
   program of the church.

6. Work with deacons, church officers, and committees as they perform their assigned responsibilities; train and lead the deacons
   in a program of family ministries.

7. Act as moderator of church business meetings.

8. Cooperate with associational, state, and denominational leaders
   in matters of mutual interest and concern; keep the church informed of denominational development; represent the church in
   civic matters.

9. Serve as chief administrator of the paid church staff; supervise the work of assigned paid staff workers.

MINISTER OF EDUCATION

PRINCIPAL FUNCTION:

The minister of education is responsible to the pastor for the development and promotion of assigned program ministries of the church.

RESPONSIBILITIES:

1. Direct the planning, organizing, conducting, coordinating, and evaluating of a comprehensive program of religious education based on program tasks.

2. Serve as a member of the church council.

3. Lead in enlisting and training volunteer workers in co-operation with the church nominating committee and Church Training.

4. Organize and direct a churchwide visitation program.

5. Serve as a purchasing agent for the church as assigned; approve and process requisitions and purchase orders.

6. Maintain personnel records of all paid staff workers; implement church-approved personnel policies.

7. Develop and promote projects such as youth camps, retreats; plan appropriate activities for senior adults.

8. Edit church publications as assigned.

9. Assist the chairmen of the various church committees; serve as exofficio member of church committees.

10. Supervise the work of assigned paid staff workers.

11. Keep informed on methods, materials, principles, procedures, promotion, and administration as related to the education program.

12. Perform other duties as assigned by the pastor; coordinate budget preparation for the assigned program ministry of the church and other assigned areas; administer the approved budget.

13. Cooperate with association and state leaders in promoting activities of mutual interest.

MINISTER OF MUSIC

PRINCIPAL FUNCTION:

    The minister of music is responsible to the pastor for the development and promotion of the music program of the church.

RESPONSIBILITIES:

1. Direct the planning, organizing, conducting, and evaluating of a comprehensive music program including choirs, vocal and/or instrumental ensembles.

2. Supervise the work of assigned paid staff workers.

3. Cooperate with the church nominating committee to enlist and train leaders for the church Music Ministry, including graded choir workers, song leaders, and accompanists for the church education organizations.

4. Lead in planning and promoting a graded choir program; direct and coordinate the work of lay choir directors; direct adult, youth, and other choirs as needed.

5. Serve as a member of the church council; coordinate the music program with the organizational calendar and emphases of the church.

6. Assist the pastor in planning all services of worship.

7. Give direction to a Music Ministry plan of visitation.

8. Arrange and provide music for weddings, funerals, special projects, ministries, and other church-related activities upon request.

9. Plan, organize, and promote choir tours, mission trips, camps, festivals, workshops, clinics, and programs for the various choirs.

10. Maintain music library, materials, supplies, musical instruments and other equipment.

11. Keep informed on music methods, materials, promotion, and administration.

12. Prepare an annual music budget for approval; administer the approved budget.

13. Cooperate with associational and state leaders in promoting activities of mutual interest.

BUSINESS ADMINISTRATOR*

PRINCIPAL FUNCTION:

The business administrator is responsible to the pastor for administering the business affairs of the church.

RESPONSIBILITIES:

1. Work with paid staff and church members to achieve the goals of the church.

2. Establish and operate an efficient plan of financial record keeping and reporting; develop bookkeeping procedures.

3. Prepare financial information for the finance and budget committees and treasurer of the church.

4. Serve as resource person regarding legal and business matters of the church; study annually the insurance program and make recommendations, if any.

5. Maintain records on church staff personnel; establish and maintain records on equipment and facilities; approve and process requisitions and purchase orders.

6. Administer church adopted policies and procedures concerning the use of all church properties and facilities.

7. Assist church building committee in its relationships with architect, contractors, and others in building, remodeling, and equipping church buildings.

8. Serve on the church council; serve as exofficio member of the deacons and church committees.

9. Work with the property and space committee preparing an annual budget of maintenance and equipment needs.

10. Supervise workers in the maintenance and repair of all physical properties; establish and implement cleaning, painting, renovating schedules; operate within approved budget.

11. Supervise the operation of food services.

12. Supervise assigned office personnel.

13. Perform other duties as assigned by the pastor.

    * Several of the duties are usually included in the minister of education's position description when the church does not have a business administrator.

MINISTER OF YOUTH

PRINCIPAL FUNCTION:

The minister of youth is responsible to the minister of education for planning, coordinating, directing and evaluating the youth educational ministry of the church.

RESPONSIBILITIES:

1. Plan, coordinate, direct and evaluate the youth ministries of the church through the youth program organizations of the church.

2. Work with youth division leaders to plan a program for leading youth to a knowledge of the plan of salvation and to develop them in Christian nurture.

3. Assist organizational leaders in the enlistment, training and guidance of youth division leaders to achieve the purposes of the church in youth education.

4. Lead in planning and conducting special age-group activities and programs appropriate for the spiritual growth of the youth of the church including Youth Week, drama, retreats, conference center meetings, camps, fellowships, banquets, mission activities, and so forth.

5. Coordinate the work of the youth division with the music and activities programs.

6. Promote a regular program of visitation for the youth division in cooperation with the overall church program of outreach.

7. Participate in the staff visitation program to prospective members, potential leaders, hospital and crisis visitation as it relates to the youth division.

8. Study and make recommendations for needed changes in the youth division such as organizational changes, space use changes, equipment and furnishings needs and policies and procedures of operation.

9. Prepare the annual budget for needs of the youth division and administer the approved budget according to policy.

10. Study new materials, programs, curriculum, educational methods, for youth and make recommendations when feasible.

11. Serve as member of the church council representing the areas of youth.

12. Visit college campuses and junior and senior high campuses for personal contact and counseling with students.

13. Maintain one-to-one contact with individual youth in all phases of the work.

14. Perform other duties as assigned by supervisor.

MINISTER OF ACTIVITIES

PRINCIPAL FUNCTION:

The minister of activities is responsible to the minister of education for leading the church in planning, conducting and evaluating a program of Christian recreation and activities for all age groups.

RESPONSIBILITIES:

1. Direct the planning, coordination, conducting and evaluation of recreational activities of the church for all ages.

2. Coordinate and administer activities in the Christian Life Center.

3. Plan and coordinate activities with all program organizations of the church so as to complement, and not conflict with, their programs.

4. Enlist and train volunteer workers to assist in the Christian Life Center.

5. Serve as recreation resource person and advisor to organizations of the church as requested.

6. Supervise all program personnel in the Christian Life Center.

7. Maintain inventory, care, repair and storage of all recreation equipment and supplies.

8. Provide representation for the church in planning, conducting, and evaluating recreation activities that involve other churches and groups.

9. Prepare and administer the approved recreation budget.

10. Prepare reports necessary for keeping the church fully informed on church activities program.

11. Work as a part of the total staff-team effort in visitation and reaching people for Christ and church membership.

12. Program the activities of the Christian Life Center to meet the overall needs of the church to develop fellowship, Christian personal growth and evangelistic outreach.

13. Work with senior adult leaders in planning and conducting their activities.

14. Perform other duties as assigned.

MINISTER OF CHILDREN'S WORK

PRINCIPAL FUNCTION:

  The minister of children's work is responsible to the minister of
  education for planning, coordinating, directing and evaluating the
  childrens' educational ministry of the church.

RESPONSIBILITIES:

  1. Enlist and train all department directors in the children's
     division; assist in enlisting and training department workers.

  2. Give guidance and coordination through enlistment, education,
     and motivation of the key leadership of children's work.

  3. Advise in the use of program materials, equipment, supplies
     and space for children groups in all church program organizations.

  4. Maintain an active program of personal witnessing and ministry.

  5. Promote a regular program of visitation for the children's
     division in cooperation with the church's plan of outreach.

  6. Provide appropriate activities for special projects; cooperate
     with the music ministry in providing music activities related
     to children.

                              of
  7. Work with the director/library services in providing resource
     materials for children's workers.

  8. Prepare an annual budget for needs of the children's division;
     administer the approved budget according to policy.

  9. Keep abreast of latest materials and methods related to children's
     work.

  10. Perform other duties as requested by the supervisor.

MINISTER OF EDUCATION AND MUSIC (Combination)

PRINCIPAL FUNCTION:

The minister of education and music is responsible to the pastor for the development and promotion of the educational and music programs of the church.

RESPONSIBILITIES:

1. Direct the planning, coordinating, conducting, and evaluating of comprehensive educational and music programs based on program tasks.

2. Supervise the work of assigned paid staff members.

3. Serve as a member of the church council.

4. Lead in enlisting and training volunteer workers in cooperation with the church nominating committee and Church Training.

5. Organize and direct a churchwide visitation program.

6. Assist the pastor in planning all services of worship; arrange and provide music for weddings, funerals, special projects, ministries and other church-related activities upon request.

7. Maintain personnel records of all paid staff workers; maintain music library, materials, supplies, musical instruments and other equipment.

8. Serve as the purchasing agent for the church as assigned.

9. Develop projects such as mission trips, festivals, youth camps, retreats; plan activities for senior adults.

10. Edit church publications as assigned.

11. Assist the chairmen of the various church committees; serve as exofficio member of church committees.

12. Prepare an annual program ministry budget for approval; administer the approved budget.

13. Keep informed on educational and music methods, materials, promotions and administration.

14. Cooperate with association and state leaders in promoting activities of mutual interest.

ORGANIST AND MUSIC ASSISTANT

PRINCIPAL FUNCTION:

    The organist and music assistant is responsible to the minister of music for serving as organist of the church and assisting in the music ministry.

RESPONSIBILITIES:

1. Play for all services of the church, both regular and special.

2. Serve as accompanist for choirs, ensembles, and soloists in regular and special rehearsals and performances, as assigned.

3. Play for weddings and funerals, as requested, and with the approval of the minister of music.

4. Assist in planning worship services, choir rehearsals, and special music events.

5. Plan and give direction to a training program designed for developing organists and pianists in the church.

6. Maintain a regular schedule of organ practice and study.

7. Serve as secretary to the minister of music; take and transcribe dictation; and maintain music ministry files, library and equipment inventories.

8. Prepare workbooks and study materials for the graded choirs, as assigned.

9. Perform other related responsibilities, as assigned.

SECRETARY

PRINCIPAL FUNCTION:

    Perform general office work in relieving supervisor of minor executive and clerical duties.

REGULAR DUTIES:

1. Take and transcribe dictation; type sermons.

2. Perform general office work; maintain supplies and various files; keep records and compile these into periodic or occasional reports.

3. Review, open, digest, and distribute mail; prepare routine answers without direction, for approval and signature; answer routine letters in absence of the supervisor.

4. Act, as required, during supervisor's absence, in making decisions or taking any necessary action not requiring supervisory approval.

5. Exercise tact, courtesy, and diplomacy in receiving callers, personal or telephone; keep calendar of appointments.

6. Notify committee members of meeting dates.

OTHER DUTIES:

7. May edit and prepare bulletin copy for printer.
9. May order literature and office supplies.
10. May assist in training new office workers.

FINANCIAL SECRETARY

PRINCIPAL FUNCTION:

Maintain the church financial records and prepare financial reports.

REGULAR DUTIES:

1. Receive, count, and deposit all church offerings.

2. Post receipts and disbursements of all accounts according to financial system.

3. Post offerings weekly to individual accounts; file envelopes.

4. Prepare bank reconciliation statements monthly.

5. Prepare monthly and annual financial reports for finance committee, deacons, and church business meetings.

6. Prepare quarterly and annual government reports.

7. Check and total all invoices when approved; inform responsible persons of their budget expenditures.

8. Receive and answer queries concerning financial matters; maintain file of invoices, correspondence and reports.

9. Prepare and issue checks to staff members, designations, and organizations, in accordance with church policy.

10. Mail pledge cards, stewardship letters, and envelopes to new members.

OTHER DUTIES:

11. Requisition and prepare all forms and records for the annual stewardship emphasis.
12. Serve in related office duties, as assigned.

STENOGRAPHER

PRINCIPAL FUNCTION:

Take and transcribe dictation and perform general office work.

REGULAR DUTIES:

1. Take and transcribe dictation.

2. Perform general office work; maintain files and supplies; keep records, and compile these into periodic reports.

3. Type copy for reproduction.

4. Receive visitors; arrange appointments and keep calendar of appointments.

5. Receive and distribute incoming mail.

6. Answer the telephone.

OTHER DUTIES:

7. May assist in mailing out the bulletin.
8. Assist in clerical work as assigned.

CLERK-TYPIST

PRINCIPAL FUNCTION:

    Maintain office files, records, and schedules; make requisitions, prepare reports, and type copy.

REGULAR DUTIES:

1. Maintain office files, program records, and schedules.

2. Fill out requisition forms.

3. Prepare reports periodically, or as directed.

4. Do routine typing and compose routine letters.

5. Correct addressograph mailing lists; operate addressograph.

6. Operate duplicating machine.

OTHER DUTIES:

7. May take and transcribe dictation.
8. May answer telephone and serve as receptionist.
9. Assist in clerical work as assigned.

TYPIST

PRINCIPAL FUNCTION:

    Type routine copy; address envelopes.

REGULAR DUTIES:

1. Type routine form letters, copy, records, record cards, and reproduction masters.

2. Address and stuff envelopes.

3. Perform routine clerical work as assigned.

OTHER DUTIES:

4. May answer the telephone.
5. May sort and deliver incoming mail.
6. May maintain addressograph file.

CHURCH HOSTESS

PRINCIPAL FUNCTION:

Oversee the operation of the kitchen and dining areas for all
food services.

REGULAR DUTIES:

1. Plan meals; purchase, prepare and serve food for all scheduled
    meals and snacks and for social functions as requested.

2. Supervise assigned personnel; enlist and direct volunteer work-
    ers; train workers in proper food preparation and service.

3. Maintain high standards of sanitation in cleanliness in cooking
    utensils, dishes, glasses, silverware, and in food handling,
    preparation, service, and so forth, and storage to assure com-
    pliance with local health and sanitation laws; maintain clean
    work areas, storage bins, and so forth.

4. Maintain accurate records in cost and operation.

5. Maintain up-to-date inventory of food supplies.

6. Arrange for the servicing, repairing and replacement of equip-
    ment in the kitchen, as needed.

7. Work with the building superintendent on table and room arrange-
    ments for all meals and social functions.

8. Assist as requested in other food services.

CUSTODIAN

PRINCIPAL FUNCTION:

Maintain clean buildings and grounds; make minor repairs.

REGULAR DUTIES:

1. Sweep, mop, buff, clean, and wax floors according to schedule; dust furniture and equipment; wash walls and windows, and vacuum carpets as scheduled.

2. Maintain clean restrooms; replenish tissue and towels; empty waste cans.

3. Request cleaning and maintenance supplies and equipment as needed.

4. Operate heating and cooling equipment according to schedule and instructions.

5. Prepare baptistry for use as directed and clean following use.

6. Open and close building daily as scheduled.

7. Mow grass; trim shrubbery, maintain clean church entrance, sidewalk, and parking areas.

8. Check with church office or supervisor daily for special assignments.

9. Move furniture, set up tables and chairs for suppers, banquets, and other similar occasions; set up assembly and classroom areas for regular activities.

OTHER DUTIES:

10. Make minor electrical, plumbing, and equipment repairs as requested.
11. Paint walls, furniture, and equipment.
12. Perform messenger service.
13. Perform other duties as assigned.

Bibliography

Will Beale, *The Work of the Minister of Education*, Convention Press, 1976.

Robert E. Bingham and Ernest Loessner, *Serving with the Saints*, Broadman Press, 1971.

Brooks R. Faulkner, *Getting On Top of Your Work*, Convention Press, 1973.

Howard B. Foshee, *Broadman Church Manual*, Broadman Press, 1973.

Howard B. Foshee, *The Ministry of the Deacon*, Convention Press, 1968.

Allen W. Graves, *A Church at Work*, Convention Press, 1972.

Lucy Renfro Hoskins, *Church Secretary: Girl Friday, Saturday, Sunday, Monday* . . .

Lucy Renfro Hoskins, *Church Secretary's Personal Enrichment Program Study Guide* (compiled) Convention Press, 1974.

Reginald M. McDonough, *Working with Volunteer Leaders in the Church*, Broadman Press, 1976.

Ernest Mosley, *Called to Joy*, Convention Press, 1973.

Idus V. Owensby, *Church Custodian's Manual*, Convention Press, 1974.

The ABC's of Church Administration (Help for the pastor who is the only staff member) Church Literature Order Form.

The Church Constitution and Bylaws, Church Literature Order Form.

The Church Council Handbook, Church Literature Order Form.

The Church Personnel Committee, Church Literature Order Form.

Leonard E. Wedel, *So You Want a Job*, Broadman Press, 1971.